AFTER *Life*

AFTER
Life

ANSWERS FROM

THE OTHER SIDE

John Edward

with Natasha Stoynoff

Princess Books
New York, NY

Copyright © 2003 by John Edward

Published in the United States by: Princess Books, a Division of Get Psych'd, Inc., New York, NY

Distributed in the United States by: Hay House, Inc., P.O. Box 5100, Carlsbad, CA 92018-5100 • (760) 431-7695 or (800) 654-5126 • (760) 431-6948 (fax) or (800) 650-5115 (fax) • www.hay-house.com • *Distributed in Australia by:* Hay House Australia Pty Ltd, 18/36 Ralph St., Alexandria NSW 2015 • *Phone:* 612-9669-4299 • *Fax:* 612-9669-4144 • www.hayhouse.com.au • *Distributed in the United Kingdom by:* Hay House UK, Ltd. • Unit 202, Canalot Studios • 222 Kensal Rd., London W10 5BN • *Phone:* 44-20-8962-1230 • *Fax:* 44-20-8962-1239 • www.hayhouse.co.uk • *Distributed in Canada by:* Raincoast • 9050 Shaughnessy St., Vancouver, B.C. V6P 6E5 • *Phone:* (604) 323-7100 • *Fax:* (604) 323-2600

Editorial supervision: Jill Kramer • *Design:* Summer McStravick

Library of Congress Cataloging-in-Publication Data

Edward, John (John J.)
    After life : answers from the other side / John Edward.
        p. cm.
    ISBN 1-932128-06-9 — ISBN 1-932128-07-7 (pbk.)
    1. Edward, John (John J.) 2. Mediums—United States—Biography. I. Title.
    BF1283.E34 A3 2003
    133.9'1'092—dc21

2003011255

Hardcover ISBN 1-932128-06-9
Tradepaper ISBN 1-932128-07-7

06 05 04 03   4 3 2 1
1st printing, September 2003

Printed in the United States of America

In memory of Charles . . .

This book has two distinctly different dedications:

For Carol Spadaro—thanks for being
the "whole army" to one 'warrior.'

And for all the skeptics/cynics:

May the White Light of the Other Side burn bright
enough to assist the spiritually blind to see. . . .

Author's note:
Portions of the transcribed readings in this book
have been edited for space and clarity.

Contents

Foreword by Larry King   ix

Acknowledgments   xi

Introduction   xv

Chapter 1:   Living on This Side   1

Chapter 2:   Shining Star Never Fades   23

Chapter 3:   Going Down Under   45

Chapter 4:   Houston   71

Chapter 5:   Telephone Tag   85

Chapter 6:   Circle of Love   111

Chapter 7:   Teachers   127

Chapter 8:   The 9/11 Factor   153

Chapter 9:   Mama Mia!   177

Chapter 10:   Papa, Can You Hear Me?   189

About the Authors   213

Foreword

JOHN EDWARD CERTAINLY IS ONE OF THE MOST EXTRAORDINARY PEOPLE I've ever known or interviewed. He has appeared on my show many, many times, and to say the least, provides fascinating TV. I'm a pure agnostic. That is, I don't know if there's a God or not, I don't know if there are other universes or not, and I certainly don't know if there's some sort of life after death.

I'll admit, John often provides insights into the departed that are not explainable. I don't know if he's seeing or hearing from the departed or if he's tuning in to the viewer's vision of the departed. I'm not even sure if there is such a thing as psychic phenomena. However, I cannot deny that John Edward often amazes.

In this, his third nonfiction book, he takes us into a further exploration of the Other Side, as he sees it. Using intimate stories from his own life, he explains how to continue relationships after this tour on Earth. Another fascinating aspect is his tour of Australia. And, naturally, the book is loaded with readings, including celebrities. We also learn of John's admitted errors, and I like the idea of a summation at the end of every chapter.

Believe him or not, you will find this book a treasure of exploration into what I call the unknown and what John calls the known. Dull, it isn't. Enjoy!

— **Larry King,** June 2003

*"The more I study the universe,
the more I believe in a Higher Power."*

— Albert Einstein

Acknowledgments

As with anything in my life, I'd be remiss if I didn't communicate my appreciation and validate my lovely wife, Sandra. Thanks for always being supportive of me and the work . . . I love you.

I also must acknowledge my three "kids": my two dogs, Jolie and Roxie, for providing me with constant unconditional love; and my beautiful li'l boy, Justin Michael, for opening up doors in my heart that I forgot were there.

To Grandma Lina and Grandpa Fernando—thanks for taking such good care of Justin.

"The Boys"—you lead, I follow . . . in this dance of spirituality.

Jon Campo, I don't have enough space here to thank you for your friendship, so always remember that there is "NO" spoon. . . .

Stacy Campo, first, we must find you an "e" for your first name. This way I stop misspelling it. ☺ First, we were all friends, and now . . . simply family.

Lydia Clar—you're still an inspiration.

Marc Chamlin, my attorney and friend, you are someone who has always been a constant in a world of variables. Thank you for your sage advice and energy.

Reid Tracy, publishing has been an evolving journey—with you as "the predicted man from the West" to be my guide. THANK YOU!

Gina Rugolo-Judd, you're the best at what you do, *and* you manage to make me laugh. Thank you for believing in me.

"Fritzarella"—a personal and private thank you. You did what only one other person in my life has ever done—and that was a college professor. She took the concept of statistics and made it easy and fun. You did that with publicity . . . thanks for becoming family.

Jack Rico—"what up, roo?" The trip to Australia would not have been the same without you acting as Barbara Walters after each seminar, dissecting each reading and questioning each moment. Thanks for your friendship. And for future reference, when a large kangaroo stands up and starts pounding its chest and flexes its muscles, it ain't bein' friendly! ☺

Natasha Stoynoff, when you approached me a few years ago and interviewed me for a few magazine stories, I knew at that time that we'd work together. Thank you for collaborating with me on this book. I hope you enjoyed the process, and becoming one of the "sitters" when you were least expecting it. I would also like to thank your other personality . . . *"Nay Tay Shay."*

Corinda Carford, you're still my publishing goddess!

Frank Sepe, your energy, sarcasm, and wit is never ending—and you're a great trainer. Thanks for your focus and time, and for pushing me to achieve my goals.

Rick Firstman, because of the time and energy you devoted to *One Last Time* and *Crossing Over,* this book now has parents. . . .

Patti Leoni—what a cook! What an energy! What a friend! Sandra and I are so happy to have met you.

Bonnie Hammer, you have been a constant supporter with honesty and friendship. Thank you!

Paul Shavelson, you drive me crazy—keep it up for many years to come.

To everyone who works so hard on *Crossing Over,* thank you for honoring the process and not succumbing to the pressures of television. You all help to share the experiences of what happens in our "gallery," and teach that life and love survive physical death. . . .

The "angels" at Media Savvy—look what you started. . . .

Isabel—if you could be cloned, we would eradicate unhappiness. And yes, they are okay!

Lucille, Joanne, Ruth, and Phil, your energy and words have helped so many of the people that I work with. Thanks for always being there.

Diane, thank you for allowing me to share your "angel" with the world.

To my Australian friends—my down-under family—I look forward to working with all of you again in the near future. Kristen, you rock! Leon . . .well, you really should be the ambassador for the country!

Steve Irwin, although I didn't get the chance to meet you personally, I really want to acknowledge the amazing work that you and your team at the Australian Zoo perform.

And while on the Aussie subject, a special thank you to the WIGGLES for managing to soothe Justin when he was cranky. All together now . . . "Hot potato, hot potato . . ."

Tricia Greenidge, thanks for taking such good care of Sandra and me when we are in "your" part of the world.

Liz Arias, a.k.a. "La Liz," thank you for always being there, here, and everywhere. . . .

Risa, no more fish photos, VIRGO! Thanks for your sense of style.

Stacey Leinson, a.k.a. "Shaloma"—your energy, enthusiasm, and professionalism are gifts. (I look forward to the first Jewish rap tour.)

Ace, Frank, John, Lance, and Marc, thanks for watching out for me.

Fran and Lowell—Mr. Leinson and Mrs. Leinson, or "Lois," as I affectionately refer to her—your escapades have kept me entertained through many of our 50 states.

Michael Logan, thanks for illuminating so many in darkness with the power of your pen.

Linda Eder, for having the voice of an angel. Your voice and music help me to relax after every event.

Whoopi . . . what can I say . . . but . . . you know!

"The 31 Club" . . . you make Wednesdays fun.

For all the energies on this side and on the Other that have helped in making this book come to life. . . .

And finally, I want to thank YOU—the person reading this—for supporting me in my quest to teach about life, love, death . . . and what comes *After Life*. . . .

Introduction

Is there something after death? Is there eternal life, as promised by certain religions? Does love transcend physical death? Are the loved ones you miss terribly still with you? And if so, are you aware that there is something *after life?*

As I worked on this book, I reflected on my career of nearly two decades as a psychic medium. I called this book *AFTER LIFE: Answers from the Other Side,* to help explain some of the lessons I've personally learned from doing this work. I initially thought that I was going to simply answer the basic questions people always ask me about this process of spirit communication. But when I sat down at my computer, it was clear that I needed and wanted to dig deeper than that and pick up where my first book, *One Last Time,* left off.

In a way, this book is kind of *One Last Time: Part II.* Even though I've written two books since that first one, many readers have told me that they resonated most with the tone, message, and sharing of intimate personal stories in that work—for example, where I described my formative years as a teenage psychic in blue jeans. Twenty years later, I'm still a psychic in blue jeans, and I'm still learning and growing.

This might be a good time to explain to newcomers who've picked up this book who I am and what I do. I'm a psychic medium who connects with loved ones who have crossed over to the "Other Side"—a place many people like to call "heaven" or "the here-after." The first question everybody asks me about this process is: How does it work? Well, basically, as a medium, I have the ability to perceive the vibrations and frequencies of those who have crossed over. Through meditation and prayer—usually with the rosary because of my Catholic upbringing—I'm able to *raise* my vibration level while the energies on the Other Side *lower* their vibrations in an effort to communicate with me.

As I've described many times, if you can imagine a helicopter propeller that moves so fast that we can't see the propellers themselves—that's how fast or high the vibrations of these energies on the Other Side are. In comparison, we on this side have a vibration more like a slowpoke ceiling fan on a hot, lazy day.

For a little while, as I speed up and they slow down, across the great divide between our two worlds we meet somewhere in the middle and communicate. The energies send me thoughts, feelings, and images—which I then relate back to the living. I always like to state right off the bat that I'm not 100-percent accurate when I relay these messages, but I do believe that the Other Side is always *completely* accurate when they deliver them. Whatever I see, hear, and feel (also known as clairvoyance, clairaudience, and clairsentience, respectively), I interpret using my own frame of reference to the best of my human abilities and perceptions.

You'll hear me describe energies coming through as being "above" (a parent, aunt/uncle, or grandparent type figure); "below" (a child); or "beside" (a contemporary—a sibling, cousin, or friend) in reference to the *sitter* (the person I'm reading—I use the term *client* and *sitter* interchangeably in this book). The genesis of these descriptions comes courtesy of my mother, who had taken it upon herself one day to research our genealogy. She sent away for one of those poster-sized charts from a catalog with a big picture of a family tree and spots for everyone's names on the branches. But when she received it in the mail, she had to laugh. The poster only had five "branches" sprouting out from the parents, and my grandmother had *11* children.

"We don't need a family tree," my mom joked, as she tucked it away behind the hope chest at the top of the stairs. "We need a family forest!" A few years later, after my mother had passed away, I was doing a reading for a client at my home and I was getting frustrated as to how to explain a male energy coming through. I felt that it was someone around the same age as the client, but I didn't know how else I could describe it. Then I looked across the room and saw a branch of that old, unused family tree sticking out from behind the chest, and the whole concept jumped out at me. I quickly said to the sitter, "To the side . . . like a brother/cousin relationship," and the woman knew who it was immediately. After the reading, I pulled out that chart and chuckled. From that day on, I started to receive my information like the branches of a family tree that stretch out above, below, and to the side.

During a reading, I rarely ask questions of the living to elicit information, which is the common argument presented by skeptics trying to explain how psychics "pull off" their so-called tricks. Instead, I *give* the information I'm getting and ask for validation. If a medium is constantly asking questions during a session, I call that "lazy mediumship." There really is a big difference between the two ways a medium can deliver the same message, which go something like this:

1st way: "Has your father passed?" (lazy medium)
2nd way: "I'm getting that your father has passed. Is that true?" (non-lazy medium)

Both mediums are receiving the same information that Dad is on the Other Side, but one sounds like he's fishing for the info while the other is stating it more as fact. When a psychic uses the lazy approach, the cynics have a field day. It gives them ammunition to jump up and yell, "See! He's getting the information from the client!" and it makes a case for refuting the validity of this work. It drives me nuts when I see a psychic who has genuine ability take the lazy route. But even I'm guilty of getting "lazy" sometimes, although I strive not to. When I catch myself giving information in question form, I give myself a nudge. I try to state the information I'm shown exactly as I see it without questions or too much editing. If a client is unable to confirm the information, I ask him or her to write it down, because one of three things is happening: (1) I misinterpreted the information I was given; (2) the sitter doesn't remember or know the information; or (3) sometimes the information I was given hasn't happened yet.

One typical example of a misinterpretation occurred while I was reading for a group, and an older male came through showing me a gun, a New York City yellow taxicab, and a younger male. I stood in front of the group insisting that someone there knew an individual who had been murdered by gunshot in a cab—that was my interpretation of what I was seeing. No one acknowledged this, but the images were clear and unrelenting.

After much frustration on my part, I finally gave the message to the group minus my angle on it: "I'm seeing a gun, a young man, and a cab. Do all these things together mean anything to anyone?" It wasn't long before someone validated that their father-in-law was coming through about his son who was shot while in the front part of a large truck—the "cab" area of the truck. I had confused both the group and myself because, first, I assumed the younger male had died from the gunshot, which he hadn't. Second, I had no idea that the front part of a truck was called the "cab," and I just figured that the gun went off in a taxi. If I hadn't relayed the information exactly as delivered, it might never have been validated.

After honing my skills doing private readings and seminars for many years, my name became highly recognizable as the host of the show *Crossing Over with John Edward,* where I conduct random readings for a gallery group in a studio. I wrote extensively about my television experiences in *CROSSING OVER: The Stories Behind the Stories,* so I won't go into detail here reiterating the behind-the-scenes scoop. Instead, for this book, I want to respond to all the letters I've received over the last few years and give you more of what you've asked for: personal and professional stories related to my interactions with the Other Side.

I BEGAN MY CAREER AS A MEDIUM after a reading with another psychic, Lydia Clar, when I was 15 years old. She'd been invited to my grandmother's home for a "psychic party," and I decided that I was going to show my very gullible family that they were being bilked by this con artist. Well, the opposite happened: I found Lydia's abilities amazing, and she changed my perspective about the world of psychic phenomena in just one session. It was at that meeting when she told me I had psychic ability and would one day be internationally known for it. I'll be turning 34 soon, and I feel that I've fulfilled Lydia's premonition of my destiny.

People always ask me what I get out of doing this work. *What's in it for me?* Well, the answer to that has changed over the years. I started off as a general psychic and was "wowed" by the fact that I could predict a person's future. Then, after two close members of my family passed on, the focus of my work shifted to mediumship and talking to the Other Side.

Often, it's the death of someone close that motivates a person to explore this subject. I'd guess that many of you readers have suffered a personal loss that inspired you to pick up this book. It was the same for me regarding my own personal development as a psychic. After the death of my uncle and my mother within two years, I needed to know they were fine and still around me. By doing readings and connecting strangers with their own loved ones, I was indirectly healing and finding closure for myself. Each time I showed someone that their mother or child was still with them, it validated for me that my family was still a part of *my* life as well. In sharing the experiences with the people who have graciously allowed me to tell their stories in this book, I hope that you, too, will find healing and closure and apply what I've learned from the Other Side to your own lives.

EVERY TIME I START TO WRITE a new book, I feel that my readers and I are like characters in *The Wizard of Oz*, traveling down that yellow brick road in search of the Emerald City and the truths behind the curtain. And at the end of our journey, we discover that life and love are eternal. And they always were . . . we just couldn't see it before.

Now . . . come with me as we follow the
yellow brick road all the way to Vegas. . . .

CHAPTER ONE

Living on This Side

LAS VEGAS, JANUARY 2002

IN LAS VEGAS YOU DON'T HAVE to be a medium to see dead people. Just take an early-morning walk through any casino and you can't help but see them at every turn. You know the type—the ones with the zombie stares and hypnotic arm lifts, dropping coins all night hoping to hit "The Big One."

Now, you might be saying, wait a minute . . . casino? . . . psychic? . . . *kaaaa-chinggggg!* It's funny to watch those serious-looking men in suits, the ones casinos pay to keep an eye out for crooked gamblers, when they recognize me at the tables. As soon as they spot me, they're watching me like hawks, trailing me from table to table, making sure I'm not using my abilities—like they're expecting me to start communing with the Other Side to find out which number is going to come up on the roulette wheel.

Well, I'm sorry to report that, at least for this psychic, being in touch with the spirit world doesn't guarantee a jackpot. And God knows I've tried—in casinos from the Caribbean to California. A long time ago, "The Boys" (the nickname I've given to my own personal spirit guides) taught me an expensive lesson—trying to cash in on my abilities will cost me big time. I remember standing in front of a roulette table many years ago getting an unmistakable vision of the number 18 in my mind—a "sure thing." I bet ten bucks on lucky number 18 and . . . lost. I bet another ten and lost again. Then another. Ten minutes and 300 bucks later, still no 18. I pulled myself away from the table and gave myself a scolding: *You know this doesn't work for you! Give it up!* But as I wandered away, I noticed everyone surrounding the table pointing and staring at me. As soon as I'd stopped betting, the roulette wheel hit 18 . . . once, twice, three times . . . six times in a row! Well, at least someone made a few bucks. So do yourself a favor . . . if you're standing next to me at a craps table sometime, don't put your money where my chips are.

But on this particular Vegas trip, I wasn't in a betting mood. I was here to work and conduct a seminar, answering questions and conducting readings for a large audience. I didn't have any sleight-of-hand tricks or a crystal ball, and I certainly can't read minds—even though that's all the cynics seem to think I'm good at. They're convinced that there's a sucker born every minute and psychics carry a bag of parlor tricks just waiting to con them. The cynics have plenty of ways to describe the methods they claim we use to fool people. They use terms like "cold reading" and "painting a bulls-eye around a lucky guess." They think we read body language, picking up facial clues or listening for voice clues. They've accused me of hiding microphones in audiences and using private detectives. I'm surprised that none of them have claimed I bug people's bedrooms to get intimate information. I haven't been accused of that one yet, but just give those cynics time!

As a medium, I've always made it a point to never try to convert anyone to my beliefs or convince anyone of my abilities. In fact, the exact opposite is true. I encourage people to be skeptical and question this process, but with an open and objective mind.

I received a letter last year from one woman who embarked on a year-long mission to expose me as a fraud. Marcia Secaur, a vice president at a major securities firm in Cincinnati, Ohio, had attended one of my seminars with a bunch of her friends on a lark.

She didn't believe in mediums and came prepared to, at the very most, have a good laugh. Instead, she ended up being shocked.

She recalled, "In a roomful of 200 people, you walked right up to a woman at the back of the room and told her she had a family member coming through who was run over by a train. And you were right."

Marcia left the seminar determined to figure out how I was tricking everybody. As someone who worked with facts, it was in her meticulous, diligent nature to get to the root of the matter—to reach the bottom line.

So she began researching the topic of mediumship—reading articles and speaking with "professional" cynics who taught her the "tricks of the trade." Then, with notebook in hand, she dissected episode after episode of *Crossing Over* to spot my con.

"I tried to take the show apart," said Marcia. "I spent a week on my couch with all my information about cold readings in front of me, and I tried to make it stick." When it didn't, she decided she had to inspect me in person. Marcia attended four seminars in a span of a few months to catch me in the act of faking it. But once again, she couldn't. So her last resort was to decide I was using a staff of detectives to dig up information about people before I read them.

"The problem with that theory," said Marcia, "was that with all the people you've worked with over the years, I couldn't believe there'd be such a vast conspiracy of silence out there that not one person would have come forward to expose."

Defeated, but not disappointed, Marcia told me that by the end of her quest, she'd become more distrustful of the cynics than of me. "It's actually the Leon Jaroffs, James Randis, and Michael Shermers of the world that frighten me," she wrote. "These are people who want to take away the comfort and peace you have given to so many people and glibly treat what you do as though it were the punch line in a bad stand-up routine. That is not practicing skepticism, it's being cruel and close minded. Discrediting you and undermining the experiences you have brought people seems more a form of entertainment for them than any noble endeavor. To attack a person's fundamental beliefs about life and death is the kind of thing wars have been fought about for centuries. Perhaps that's why your guides say you will have the role of warrior in regard to your field."

Warrior or not, it's not my job to change people's minds, and it's not my business to prove that what I say is true. I'll never defend what I believe in or what I do. If I did, I'd be admitting that there's something to defend—and there simply isn't.

My role is to be a bridge between our world (the physical) and the spirit world (the nonphysical), and to deliver messages from the Other Side to the living. But often that's easier said than done. There are times when I receive, interpret, and pass on a message to the person I'm reading and the information is easily validated. But there are also times when I get something and the person I'm reading doesn't understand the information right away.

Or, in some cases, the message might not even be intended for the person I'm talking to—but for another relative, a friend, or acquaintance who isn't present during the session. This type of message might not get validated immediately, and in some cases it might take weeks or even months for the validation to occur. I call those validations "Aha!" moments, a phrase I coined many years ago because I saw this delayed validation scenario happen so often. I can't count how many times I've passed on information to a sitter that they didn't understand, only to get a phone call the next day saying something like, "I just checked with my mom, and I didn't know this, but she *did* have an Aunt Gertrude who died in a plane crash over the Amazon. . . ." Or even, "Oh, that 'Thomas' you kept mentioning? It didn't hit me that you could mean my *brother* Tom. . . . "

This is what is also known as "psychic amnesia," another phrase I coined that means the complete and sudden deterioration of your memory when a medium is talking to you. You forget how and when your relatives passed, you forget their names, your own name . . . I've seen it happen time and time again.

Sometimes the person the message is for just isn't paying attention—even if that person happens to be a seasoned psychic medium like yours truly. . . .

IT HAPPENED IN VEGAS on an unusually crisp January afternoon. More than 2,000 people had turned up at the banquet hall at the MGM Grand Hotel hoping to get messages from their loved ones who had crossed over. Many of them *did* get messages, but the one that came through strongest was the one I received myself—and it would change my life forever. It was an earth-shattering "Aha" moment of my own and, just like I've seen it happen to others, it took me weeks to figure out.

I walked onto that Vegas stage and, despite the huge crowd, felt right at home. There were a few familiar faces in this audience who had known me since I was a kid and had come to see "little Johnny" all grown up. One of them was my good friend and fellow psychic, Virginia, who came to cheer me on. Try to picture Judge Judy as a psychic and you've got Virginia: a real no-nonsense type. I also spotted my Uncle Carmine's sister, Loretta, and her family and friends. (For those of you who read *One Last Time,* you might remember that I talked about Uncle Carmine and the premonition I had about his very young passing from a heart attack.)

The air was charged with the usual electricity that often fills a room just before I do a group reading. Everyone is excited and nervous, wondering, *Will someone come through for me? Who will it be? What will they tell me?*

But whether it's Vegas or Vermont, readings are always a gamble, a crapshoot. Sometimes I feel as if those who attend an event are like players in a poker game, laying down those hard-earned chips and praying they'll get the right card. Hopefully, they walk away without being too disappointed if it wasn't their lucky night.

But I like to think that everyone comes away a winner.

I often explain that a group reading is like a birthday party. Imagine that you're a kid and it's your birthday—there's a cake in front of you loaded down with glowing candles and your name across the top in big, loopy letters. But just because it's *your* party and those are *your* candles marking *your* special day, it doesn't mean this is a private celebration. Every person at the party will get a slice of your cake and come away with a goodie bag. The same holds true with a reading for a large group of people. If the seminar is a party and the reading is the cake—even if the cake isn't specifically yours with your name on it, but is intended for another person or family, you still get a slice of it just by being at the party. Because you're listening and taking part, the reading is just as much for you (conceptually) as it is for the other person. So you go home with the goodie bag—the knowledge that life and love are eternal.

That night in Vegas, I was about to get an amusing lesson in birthday-party etiquette from the Other Side. I knew that I had a big cake to divvy up, but I had no clue that it had my name on it.

The trip had already started off on a strange note. You see, my wife, Sandra, decided to accompany me. Not that that's a bad thing, but she usually doesn't want to come on these tours. When I'm on the road, I'm usually booked to appear in several cities in a very short time period. It's always a hectic schedule, so there isn't much time to do anything except rush to the airport, hop on a plane, check in to a hotel, and then do the seminars. There might be time for a quick bite afterwards and maybe a fast workout if I'm lucky, then a few hours sleep and up early to do it all over again.

It can go on like that for days, so I usually discourage Sandra from coming along because, quite honestly, when she's there I can get a little distracted—worrying if she's bored and trying to make sure she's having a good time. But this time, she wanted to be there . . . and I don't believe anything is ever a coincidence. The Other Side had a message for both of us.

HOLLYWOOD AND WHINE

SANDRA AND I DECIDED TO SPEND A COUPLE OF DAYS IN L.A. to squeeze in a mini-vacation before my hectic work schedule kicked in. We planned to meet with a few friends and do a little sightseeing, shopping, and "stargazing." On one of the nights we were there, the Golden Globe Awards happened to be taking place, and we were invited to go to one of the after-parties. Now, I usually don't like to attend these "Hollywood" things because of all the fuss that goes along with it, but I must admit that I'm as excited as the next fan to meet the celebrities I admire.

I remember a few years ago when I caught sight of my favorite singer, Linda Eder, on 6th Avenue through the glass of the restaurant where I was having lunch. Next thing I knew, I was racing through the crowded street and pushing aside pedestrians like a quarterback running for the end zone. I caught up to her on the sidewalk and babbled something charming and intelligent like, "OhMy-GodAreYouLindaEder?" and told her that I'd been her biggest fan since her early days on *Star Search*. I handed her my card, which read "John Edward—Psychic Medium" and asked her if she could include my name on any mailing list she might have for upcoming concerts. She looked at my card, then back at me, perplexed.

"Um . . . or if you're ever interested in speaking with any of your dead loved ones," I added, "please give me a call!" (Note: She never did. Then two years later I attended her concert at the PNC Arts Center in New Jersey and had the chance to go backstage afterward. In a room crammed full of people, I was trying to hang back . . . hoping Linda wouldn't recognize me as the weirdo who'd chased her down 6th Avenue. But when Linda's publicist ushered me forward to introduce me, Linda said I looked familiar. "Oh, he's that *stalker fan* you met on the street a few years ago!" Sandra chimed in.)

So I'm not immune to the lure of stargazing once in a while, and this Golden Globes party would definitely be wall-to-wall stars. So what would keep me from a star-studded event like this? Three words: the press line. See, I don't consider myself a celebrity. Yeah, I'm on TV and people recognize me at the supermarket and at the mall. But the truth is, I don't do what I do to gain fame. I do it to help people. It's an ability I've been given, and I want to share it with as many people as I can. Being on television and touring the country doing seminars allows me to do that. But I'm just not a Hollywood type of guy, and photographers snapping my picture and reporters sticking microphones in my face just unnerves me.

No offense to any reporters reading this—you're just doing your job. It's not you, it's me. I have no problem getting up in front of thousands of strangers and bringing through loved ones from the

Other Side . . . energies who often send me very intimate and potentially embarrassing messages. I pass the juicy details along for all the world to hear without much wavering. If you want to talk to me about my work, I'm fine. But put me in front of a TV camera to talk about myself and I become a ball of nerves . . . because then it's about me the *person* and not me the medium.

When it comes right down to it, I'm really a shy guy who has purposely stayed in the background most of my life. Anyone who knew me growing up can attest to the fact that I never wanted to be "known" or "famous"—quite the contrary. I never liked being in the forefront of anything, whether it was in school or on the job. My biggest dream as an adolescent was to own my own deli. After that, it was to be behind the scenes in the health-care field. To this day, I'm just a few credits short of my master's degree in health-care administration. (As parents say, "It's something to fall back on.") So for me, to be thrust in front of the spotlight has had its uncomfortable moments.

Okay, okay . . . I know what you're thinking (and not because I'm psychic). *Poor John. He has his own TV show, chitty-chats with Larry King on CNN, and gets invited to stroll down the red carpet into star-studded parties . . . and all he can do is complain?!* Believe me, the person playing the air-violin the loudest is my lovely wife, Sandra, who enjoys attending these glittery affairs. So when we landed in L.A. with invites to the Golden Globes party in our suitcase, Sandra was raring to go, and she wasn't about to hear me whine about having to walk past a few eager shutterbugs to get there. That's why what happened next seemed all the more strange.

As I mentioned, Sandra was excited about the party, so she went out and bought a new outfit and could talk about nothing else during the entire trip out to L.A. The night of the party, she spent hours getting ready, but I have to admit, it was all worth it. She looked incredible—glowing, in fact. She was wearing a strapless evening gown and these sexy shoes that tied up around her ankles.

We headed off to the party with Sandra anticipating the celebrities we were likely to see. Now most people would have hired a limo—or at least a driver in a town car—to take them to the event.

But this would have attracted too much attention for my taste. Instead, I rented a car so we could pull up to the side and slip in to the party unnoticed. When I turned onto Santa Monica Boulevard and got close to the famous Trader Vic's restaurant, where the party was being held, it looked like a paparazzi convention. I looked at Sandra, said "No way," and kept driving.

Five long L.A. blocks later, I found a parking spot, which meant that Sandra had to walk a half mile in those new, skinny heels. She didn't say much—but I knew that she wasn't a happy camper. By the third block, she'd decided to break her silence and let me know exactly what she thought about my parking plan . . . let's just say she wasn't entirely pleased. She was feeling tired, her feet were killing her, and we had to stop half a dozen times so she could hike up her gown and retie those shoes.

When we got to Trader Vic's, I guided Sandra toward a side entrance, sneaking past the media mob, where we bumped into a tall, stone-faced security guard who asked to see our passes.

"Security passes?" I asked.

Right. I knew exactly where they were. They were sitting on the end table back at the hotel.

"Ah . . . go ahead, I know who you are," the security guard said, and waved us in with a smile of recognition. "What's the matter? Didn't anyone up there remind you to bring them?" Heh, heh. Phew . . . thanks to my "celebrity" status, we were quickly moving down an empty hallway headed straight to the party. If we were turned away from the door because I forgot those security passes, Sandra would have never let me hear the end of it. She was still miffed about our hike from the car, but once we got to the party she forgot all about it. There were stars from our favorite TV shows and movies everywhere we looked—Benjamin Bratt, Andie Mac-Dowell, Maggie Smith, Josh Hartnett. I was glad we'd come and was anxious to start mingling.

We'd been there just under an hour when Sandra—AKA Miss Party Animal—turned to me and said she was tired and wanted to leave.

"But . . . but . . . Will and Grace are over there, two feet from us . . . and you want to leave?" I protested.

"If we don't leave this minute," she said, "I'm gonna crawl over there, curl up on Will and Grace's laps, and go to sleep. . . . "

I'd never known Sandra to want to cut out of a good party—let alone one set in a galaxy of stars. But as soon as we were back in the room, she hit the sack and was out like a light. I figured that the traveling and the time difference had really knocked her out.

IS THERE A PSYCHIC IN THE HOUSE?

THE NEXT DAY WE WERE OFF TO VEGAS and back to work. Sandra kept busy at the seminar handling one of the microphones, running up and down the aisles and squeezing between the rows of people in the audience, making sure everyone could hear each other during the Q&A period and the readings. The validations were coming through nice and easy until one of the last readings of the day when I was pulled to the back of the hall. When I say "pulled," I don't mean someone—living or dead—was physically grabbing ahold of me and dragging me. It's not a physical pull; it's an *energy* pull. I feel like I'm being tethered by an invisible line of energy from my sternum leading directly to where the message must be delivered. Whether I'm reading a group of 12 or 12,000, it's the same feeling.

On the television show *Saturday Night Live,* comedian Will Ferrell does a really funny parody of me being "pulled" all over the place, kind of like a frenetic cross between Jim Carrey and Gumby. I'm the first one to laugh at it—and myself—folks. The other thing people like to kid me about is how during a reading I can turn into a pit bull. I'll sink my teeth into a bit of information coming through and not let it go until someone validates it. And if the person can't validate it after much persistence on my part, I make them write it down to check later, hopefully for an "Aha" moment to come.

So on this night, I was pulled toward the back of the room. I sensed a female energy coming through "from above," like a grandmother, and had a strong feeling there was a young woman in that section who had recently lost her grandma . . . or at least, there was someone sitting there who was *connected* to a young woman who just lost her grandmother. When no one put up their hand, I explained to the audience that this girl didn't have to be in the room, but could just be linked to a person who was present. I told them that if anyone had a relative, friend, or co-worker who was not with them today and their grandmother had passed within the last few weeks, they should please put up their hand. Sandra, who was standing in the back of the hall, looked around, ready to take the microphone to the person who could acknowledge this message.

Nada.

The next message came through loud and clear. Somehow connected to this girl with the deceased grandmother was another girl in the room who was pregnant.

A hush came over the room.

Now, one of my favorite things about this work is watching the similarities in people's reactions all over the country when I make certain statements. Whenever I announce that someone in the room is pregnant, no one wants to put her hand up. It's as if I'm handing out some sort of horrific diagnosis—no one seems to want it. This day was no different. Someone was pregnant, but she wasn't about to own up to it. After I spent about 15 minutes delivering this same message over and over . . . the grandmother . . . the pregnancy . . . I just thought, *Wow . . . some woman is soooooo pregnant and maybe she doesn't know it yet. Surprise, surprise!*

But I was starting to get frustrated, too. Okay, maybe you don't know you're pregnant, or you don't want to tell hundreds of strangers that you are, and that's fine. But why was no one acknowledging a grandmother who'd recently passed? The problem with a message not being validated in a big group is that during the long pauses in the session, other energies trying to connect with their own family will jump in and try to take over. They see an opening and grab it. And that's exactly what happened in this case. While waiting for the grandma and the pregnant woman to show themselves, I saw a flash of steel bars in front of me.

"I'm seeing bars," I told the audience. "To me, this means someone may have a relative in prison or was in prison, and this

might be connected as well. Does someone back there understand that?"

Shake of heads. If this had been baseball, I'd be batting zero.

I now had the pregnancy, the grandmother, and someone else's
family (I thought) coming in with some type of incarceration issue.
And nobody was fessing up to any of it. I could see it was going to
be a long night.

This back-and-forth went on for at least a half hour. This was
really getting to me, but I assumed my pit-bull stance, planted my
feet solidly and squarely apart, dug in my heels, and stood my
ground. I wasn't going anywhere until we figured this out. Whoever was coming through wasn't giving up either, so I asked the
grandmother figure for help—literally. When I say this, I mean I
actually asked her for help. I silently urged her in my mind, *Ya gotta
give me something more to work with here. Give me a detail someone will
recognize.* Well, she did. She told me she was connected to the initial "J," as in Joanne or Josephine. (Again, just to explain the
process, it's not that I'm *seeing* this granny in front of me. What I
was actually seeing was my own grandmother in my mind's eye,
which always signifies to me that it's a grandmother coming
through. Then, I could hear the "JJJJJ" sound in my head.)

Still, of the 2,000 people in the room, no one claimed this
grandma who was working really hard to come through. And
here's where I laugh at what the cynics say about this process.
According to them, all these gullible, stupid people are just hanging on to my every word, waiting and hoping with bated breath to
pounce on whatever far-fetched information I'm giving so they can
yell, "Yessss, it's meeeee!" because they're so desperate to believe
anything. Well, the cynics would be hard-pressed to describe anyone in this audience as jumping on that message.

I began to get impatient with whoever in the audience could
not, or rather, would not, validate this message. Again, you'd know
if your grandmother just passed, right? And if you had a friend
whose name began with a "J" like Joanne or Josephine who just lost
her grandmother, you'd remember that. Maybe I was dealing with
a severe case of psychic amnesia. By this point, I was positive that

the woman who was pregnant was in the room, and was in the area I was being pulled toward. Then I got another detail . . . an image of my wife and singer Ricky Martin.

"The person this is connected to is a huuuuuuggge Ricky Martin fan," I told the group, "and I know this because they're showing me a picture of my wife, Sandra, and a picture of Ricky Martin!"

My friend Liz, who also has a teenybopper obsession with the magnetic Mr. Martin, was on microphone duty that day. She started to tease Sandra in the back of the room, saying, "Maybe it's you he's talking about . . . Ricky Martin fan, back of the room, and he saw your face. Maybe it's you!"

Sandra laughed. "Yeah, right . . . " and continued to look around to see if anyone would own up to this reading. After much frustration, I had to give up. I guess the pregnant woman with the dead grandmother and the hots for Ricky Martin just wasn't ready to come forward.

ESP vs. EPT

ON THE FLIGHT BACK TO NEW YORK, our friends continued to tease Sandra and me that the "unclaimed" message was for us, but we laughed it off. We were getting ready for the family-planning phase of our lives together, it's true, but we hadn't officially begun the *trying* phase yet so . . . no way. It wasn't us.

A week later, it was the anniversary of my grandfather's death—and also his wife's—my grandmother Josephine's—birthday. The day is always filled with a lot of emotion for the family, and every year we have a Catholic mass in their honor and a get-together afterward at my grandmother's old house in Glen Cove, Long Island. That was the house I grew up in, which is now my Aunt Roseann's home.

As the usual cast of lively characters of aunts, uncles, and cousins in my big Italian family sat around the table and reminisced about one thing or another, I started daydreaming, glancing up at the walls at the old family photos hanging there. Everywhere I looked, I saw reminders of my childhood and of the family parties gone by. It was such a feeling of "home" for me. As I continued to study the photos, I was drawn to the portrait of my mom hanging on the wall, and I felt a weird twinge. Time seemed to freeze. It was as if all my relatives on the Other Side suddenly wanted to make their presence known to me in a major way, like I was getting my own reading with my entire family. I glanced at the photos, then over to Sandra . . . and it hit me.

Aha!

The second we left the house, walking down the driveway, I blurted it out: "You're pregnant!" Sandra looked at me like I was crazy.

In any case, we drove right over to the local Glen Cove CVS pharmacy—directly across the street from the strip mall where I worked in my teens, and bought a pregnancy kit. When we got home, Sandra ran to the bathroom while I let our dogs, Jolie and Roxie, outside. By the time I brought the dogs back in, Sandra was standing in the hallway, holding up the little blue stick.

"It's positive." She smiled. "We're pregnant!"

Now Sandra's fatigue at the Golden Globes party made sense. And so did the messages in Vegas. The Ricky Martin fan, the picture of Sandra, the pull to the back of the room, the pregnancy . . . was all for *us*. Seems I'd hit the Vegas jackpot after all. But there was one thing that didn't make sense. Who was the grandmother who'd just passed connected to the "J" name? Who was our kindly messenger? The answer would reveal itself shortly.

JOANNE GETS CALLED TO THE OFFICE

BOTH SANDRA AND I HAD LOST OUR GRANDMOTHERS a few years earlier, so we knew that this grandma didn't belong to us. We were perplexed. But I knew that this older woman had to belong to someone Sandra or I was connected to. Here she was, good enough to bring us our news, and I had no clue how to let her family know that she'd come through. Then my friend Liz, who's also the supervising producer on *Crossing Over,* remembered something. Our post-production supervisor, Joanne, had recently lost her grandmother. Liz insisted that we call Joanne and quiz her about it. But I started to wonder . . . could I have misinterpreted the message? Could it have been *my* grandmother, Josephine, coming through?

Liz was insistent that the message was for Joanne. (Liz has great intuition, and I always tease her about it, saying she's not allowed to have her own show called *Crossing Over with La Liz.*)

"John, you're being a relative stealer," Liz accused me, referring to how I describe audience members who insist information is coming through for them when it's not. "You don't like it when people do it in the gallery, and now you're doing it yourself!" Liz had paid very close attention to the details of that session in Vegas and was determined to find the true recipient.

"The grandmother was connected to the 'J' name," she corrected me. "She herself wasn't the 'J' name. Remember?"

Of course I didn't remember. When I do readings, it's as if the images and impressions are downloaded into me from the Other Side like a computer downloads onto a disk. The thoughts don't originate in my own brain, so I rarely remember them afterwards.

"And," Liz added, "Joanne's grandmother just passed away."

Before I could protest anymore, Liz called Joanne and began interrogating her on speakerphone. Had her grandmother passed? *Yes, about a week before.* And . . . um . . . don't mean to pry . . . but did she happen to have a family member in jail? Joanne had no idea about that one. And, if we didn't mind, why were we asking?

"We can't explain just now," I spoke up, "but can you check it out?" Poor Joanne—we probably freaked her out. She made some frantic phone calls to her mother and her aunt and called back within 15 minutes to let us know, in a surprised and slightly trembling voice, that, yes, as a matter of fact, she did have a relative in jail. . . .

"Get over to John's office right away," Liz told her. *Click.*

The post-production facility for the show, where Joanne supervises the editing, was just around the corner from my office, but she must have sprinted anyway because when she arrived a minute and a half later, she was gasping for breath and looking queasy. Actually, she looked terrified. She expected me to give her some sort of tragic family news—and who could blame her?

"No, no . . . don't worry," I told her. "We actually might have good news for you." I sat her down in a chair so her knees would stop shaking, and started to relay the story slowly, step by step, so I wouldn't shock her or anything.

"Joanne, I understand your grandmother just passed. . . . "

"Yes . . . "

"Well, when we were in Vegas, we had a grandmother come through at the seminar . . . "

"Okay . . . "

"She came through with the news that Sandra was pregnant . . . "

"Wow . . . cool . . . "

"And she was connected to a 'J' name."

"Uh-huh."

"Maybe a 'Joanne.' We think it was your grandmother. "

A look of total relief washed over Joanne's face. "You're kidding!" she squealed. We described the rest of the reading, detail by detail, and Joanne agreed that it was her grandma. But strangely enough, of all the emotions Joanne was feeling at that moment, surprise wasn't one of them. With a triumphant smile on her face, she told us why her grandma Anne, who'd passed away at 91 from Lou Gehrig's disease, had made such a timely appearance.

"On the last night of my grandmother's wake, a week before, all of my cousins brought photos and different things to put in the casket with her . . . but I didn't have anything. I'd gone through all my photos of us together the night before, and I wanted to keep all of them, so I was very upset that I didn't have anything to put in. Then my mother said to me, 'Why don't you put in one of your *Crossing Over* business cards?' I took one out and, because my grandmother always used to kiss our birthday cards with a big lipstick kiss, I kissed the back of the card with a big lipstick kiss myself. And with a pen I wrote on the back: 'I love you, Grandma. Please go to John!' I tucked the card under her vest, over her heart, and I never told anybody about it."

Liz and I were floored by Joanne's story and were glad that the mystery grandma had finally been identified.

"We've spent days trying to figure this out," Liz told her. "John's been driving me crazy ever since Thursday."

Joanne got a funny look on her face.

"Thursday? Did this happen Thursday of last week?"

We nodded.

"What time?"

Now it was our turn to be curious. We told her it had happened around 7 P.M. Vegas time, and Joanne jumped up out of the chair and shrieked.

"Oh my God! That night, right around that time, I was looking at a picture of my grandmother on the fireplace mantel, and I was thinking that both my grandmothers were gone. I got very upset and cried, and I just looked up at the sky and said out loud, again, 'Grandma, please go to John!'"

Okay, now I was turning into mush, and all three of us were grinning from ear to ear.

"Well, that explains the timing of it all," I told her. "But I still wonder . . . of all the information your grandmother could have come through with, why would she choose to talk about Sandra's pregnancy?"

Joanne thought about this for a minute and remembered something.

"Maybe my grandmother was repaying a good deed," she explained. "My aunt was sitting in the gallery watching a taping of *Crossing Over* a few months ago, and John had told her that in January there was going to be a big event—a celebration—in her family, and that my uncle, who had passed six months earlier, was going to be there for it. And then John got a number five attached to it. As it turned out, in January, after many years of trying, my cousin was able to adopt a baby. They signed the papers and brought the baby home on January 5th. It was a really big to-do for the family. Maybe my grandmother was repaying John. He'd brought us news about my cousin's baby, and she was now bringing him news of his *own* baby."

That worked for us. I loved the whole circularity of it all.

And so, I found out I was going to be a dad from my co-worker's deceased grandmother, whom I'd never known in life. It was a validation that neither Joanne nor I will ever forget. And it's a good example of how the Other Side has its own reasoning and rationale about the way a message comes through. I would have expected a relative of mine to come through to deliver baby news like that rather than a complete stranger—that would have been the logical route for them to take. But the Other Side is not logical in human terms; they operate on their own agenda and are much wiser than we are. This way, I got my news, and at the same time, a co-worker received validation that her grandmother was alive and well on the Other Side. Someone else might have been disappointed that Grandma didn't have a specific message for her, but Joanne knew her big message was just that her grandmother came through as requested in spite of the fact that Joanne wasn't even in the room.

So often, energies come through when they know someone in the room can pass on the message to a loved one. I can't count how many times a person has come for a session, and on their way to my office a co-worker jokingly mentions, "Hey, say hi to my Aunt Susan who passed away last year!"

Well, wouldn't you know it, Aunt Susan shows up in the middle of the reading. Or, to your dismay, she takes up your *entire* reading. And then you have to go back and report all the details to your buddy because the reading ended up being for her.

We actually did an entire episode of *Crossing Over* (called "Being the Messenger") on this very phenomenon. It was full of very moving accounts of readings I did for people who weren't even in the studio. But their friend/relative/co-worker or acquaintance was there, and they had to scribble down every word I said so they could pass it on.

It's not such an easy task—being the "spiritual mail carrier"!

IT'S A GIRL—NOT!

THE OTHER SIDE WASN'T THROUGH WITH ME just yet.

Throughout her pregnancy, Sandra and I were toying with whether or not we should find out if the baby was a boy or girl. For all of you who are asking, why I, a psychic, would have to ask a doctor . . . well, predicting the sex of a child for me is like predicting the next card at the blackjack table—it's not my strong suit. This specialty was my mother-in-law, Lina's, domain, who's about 95-percent accurate in predicting the sex of a baby just by looking at the mother. Her prediction for us was that we were going to have a girl, and that was her final answer. So, we all planned on a girl. We were struggling to come up with female names we could agree upon, but only seemed to agree on a boy's name—Justin. We kept joking that it would be a lot easier if it was just a boy, since we already had the name.

The night before we were due to have the second-level sonogram, I had a dream that I was wrestling with Roxie, one of my two bichon frise pooches. During this dream, she morphed into a fat baby wearing a stinky diaper that needed to be changed, and in the dream, I changed the diaper. And lo and behold, the "she"-baby was most definitely a "he." At three o'clock in the morning, I leaned over and woke Sandra up to tell her that "Muffina," as I was affectionately calling the baby, was now going to have to be called "Muffin-o" because we were having a boy. I was sure that my psychic dream would override my mother-in-law's old-world maternal instincts. But even after this revelatory dream, Lina was still insistent that it was a girl. And so was everyone else, even though the psychic in the house begged to differ. Well, you should have seen the look on Sandra's face when the technician told her we were indeed having a boy. Lina was sure the doctors were all wrong until the day Justin Michael was born.

LABOR DAY

JUSTIN, AS WE KNEW HIS NAME WOULD BE, didn't like the concept of being upside down and would not turn to make a natural delivery possible. The doctors decided that Sandra would have to have a cesarean section—something she was not at all opposed to after the last sonogram told us our baby would be a big, strapping eight-plus pounds.

"We're going to schedule the cesarean for next Tuesday," the doctor told us.

I shook my head. No way.

Now, imagine if you will, that you're an obstetrician and your patient's husband tells you he doesn't want to have the baby on a specific date because of the child's astrological chart. Actually, I should clarify here; Sandra was ready to have him pronto, right in the doctor's office—that's how ready she was. But I really wanted Justin to be a Libra, like Daddy. Since the baby and Sandra were in no danger and there was an opening in his schedule the following week, the doctor agreed to change the date by a couple of days to please me. But I'm sure he was thinking all the while: *These people are nutty!*

The delivery date was now going to be September 25th (the Libra sun sign begins on the 23rd). We checked into the hospital with quiet excitement, knowing that in a few short hours our lives would be changed forever. As the doctors prepared for surgery and Sandra was wheeled into the operating room for pre-surgical procedures, I was out in the hall in a surgical gown and mask, preparing for the big event.

I expected, of course, that all of my relatives from the Other Side were going to show up. I was positive that my mother, grandmother, uncle, aunt, and other family and friends would be right there with me when Justin came into the world so they could be the first to congratulate us. It was going to be standing room only in this delivery room!

Out in the hall, I prayed the rosary and meditated as if I were preparing for an uber-marathon reading session. I did my special breathing exercises with the visualization that all would go exactly as planned. And when they called me into the delivery suite, I was serene, prepared, and confident. I looked at my beautiful wife, knowing that something out of this world was about to happen.

And that's when it happened.

Nothing! At least, not from the Other Side.

In front of me, on this side, plenty was happening—my son was being born. But why wasn't I getting anything from the Other Side? I sharpened my psychic tuning fork and put my faculties on high alert. Nothing. I neither heard, felt, nor saw a thing.

Meanwhile, Sandra was busy becoming a mother and wondering where the heck I was. She looked over at me with such love that, in an instant, I was brought back to this world.

And what proceeded from there was truly wondrous. I became a dad and watched the miracle unfold right in front of me as my little boy arrived into the world.

But I won't lie and tell you that I wasn't disappointed that no vision, thought, flash, or feeling was downloaded to me from my family on the Other Side. Part of me was borderline devastated. At that moment, I fully understood how my clients feel when they don't get what they're looking for from a reading.

It was strange to feel such extreme emotions at once—total joy at holding my son for the first time, yet total sadness that my mother wasn't "with me" when my first child was born. I felt kind of deserted by her and let down by my guides. Was it too much to ask if just once I could get a validation of my own in the way I'd envisioned it? It took me a minute or two to shake off the self-pity as I gave myself an imaginary slap on the wrist for doing exactly what I tell my clients not to do: expect the Other Side to serve us like we're at a restaurant ordering a meal.

I looked up at my wife's smiling face and realized an important lesson: We can't get caught up with the spiritual world and forget to pay attention to the physical world—to what's right in front of us. We can't constantly look for validations from the Other Side every step we take or we'll miss all the little joys of life on this side. We're here for a reason—to live our lives as best we can and to be as fully present in our lives as possible. We have to appreciate the validations as they come . . . in their own way.

Once I got that, then the validation *did* happen. But not in the way I expected it. As the doctors, nurses, and technicians were finishing up all their individual tasks, they began discussing the rest of their day. It was informal banter among colleagues, but one by one, in their conversation, they began unknowingly naming all my family members who had passed that I hoped would be there.

"Oh, look at him," said one of the technicians, gazing at Justin. "You had a little boy! So you got a prince instead of a little princess!" "Princess" was my mother's nickname, and every time I hear it or see it written, it's a hello from mom.

"Hey, Rachel, can you pass me the . . ." Rachel was my aunt. Josephine, my grandmother, was then mentioned, and within two minutes, three other family members were named out loud in succession. Coincidence? I don't think so. The Other Side has their own agenda and their own way. I tell people that over and over all the time. The mere acknowledgment of my family's names in that passing conversation was validation enough for me that they were there in the delivery room, sharing my joy.

CHAPTER TWO

Shining Star Never Fades

EVERY NOW AND AGAIN, I meet up with people who think they're being funny—and original—by asking me if I've talked to Elvis lately. With the recent release of Elvis's number-one hits CD, I had a ton of radio stations calling me up, trying to book me on their shows so I could get them an exclusive "interview" with Elvis from the Other Side. And that request was one of the more *sincere* ones. Some of the others were way out there—even for a guy who talks to the dead.

But even if I *did* connect with Elvis, I wonder if his fans would be disappointed. Would he still be "The King" on the Other Side? I often advise people not to expect their loved ones to be *exactly* as they were when they were here in the physical world. There's a process we go through—a shedding of the Earthly world that we leave behind—that's part of the transition. When we shed our bodies, our worldly limitations disappear . . . our physical weaknesses are gone, and our emotional burdens dissolve. It's like the worm going into the cocoon, shedding skin, and becoming the butterfly. We *are* that worm as we move through life, and one day we become that butterfly when our physical body dies, allowing our soul to soar.

Don't get me wrong—your loved ones' personalities will be intact when they connect with you either through a medium or through your own experience. You'll definitely be able to recognize them and know that they're still connected to you. But there are also times when they'll come through to you and seem different from what you remember. I like to believe that the reason for the change is that transition, that shedding—and now they see life from a different perspective. For example, if someone was extremely prejudiced in life, I'm positive that upon their transition that type of mind-set *has* to change. I was shown by my guides many years ago that we're all wearing an invisible coat with many pockets. Pockets of love, fear, disappointment, and judgment line this coat, and when we cross over, part of our transition is to empty out those pockets and examine their contents—whether positive or negative—as part of our soul's progression. In time, once we fully understand our "pocket" issues, they become embedded in the fabric of our soul and we take off the coat.

As this progression occurs, our spirit changes. Our negative issues soften, and our positive issues are highlighted. So if you've had a psychic experience where a loved one came through and their personality seemed different to you, this might be why.

Shortly after my mom crossed over, she came to me in a dream, but not just a regular dream. It was a very vivid experience, and so real that I remembered every last detail when I awoke. The details stayed with me for years afterward. This is how I know it was more than a dream, more than a manifestation of my subconscious. This was a "visit." A visit is when someone who has crossed over connects with us in our dreams. It's the number-one way for an energy to come through to a human being. Why? Because in the dream state, we accept the experience more readily—it's "safer."

When most people are visited by a loved one in a dream, it doesn't scare or confuse them, as opposed to what would happen if all of a sudden their deceased mom appeared at the foot of their bed in broad daylight. In a dream, we have the luxury of rationalizing that "it was just a dream," while at the same time, actually experiencing a bona fide visit.

In the dream/visit I had with my mother, I kept asking her to tell me what to do about a certain frustrating situation I was going through at the time, but all she would do was smile, tell me that she loved me, and remind me that she was there for me. Being the relentless person I am, I wasn't satisfied with such a fluffy, angelic-type response, and I kept trying to pin her down to a more definite answer. She finally told me that those on the Other Side aren't allowed to tell us what to do because we're here to learn specific lessons for our own soul's growth, and they can't interfere with our learning or take on the responsibility for our actions. And then she told me again that she loved me, and blah, blah, *blah*. . . .

When I woke up, I was really ticked off. If my mother were alive, she wouldn't have wasted a second telling me exactly what she thought about the situation and what do to about it—and she would have more than likely kicked my ass for finding myself in that situation anyway. (For curious readers out there wondering about my predicament, it's nothing juicy enough for me to go into detail about. But for a 20-year-old who had just lost his mother, who was trying to take on the financial responsibilities she'd left behind, and who was taking care of his grandmother and aunt as well, my plight seemed disastrous at the time.) During my visit, it was as if my mother had undergone some type of Stepford-Mom personality transplant and a flower-power energy had taken over to scatter tulips for me to tiptoe through. I had to realize that with her new knowledge and experiences on the Other Side, there would also be a new side to my mother.

So, what about Elvis? JFK (Sr. and Jr.)? Princess Diana? Mother Teresa? Or even Hitler? All these larger-than-life individuals are no longer the exact same energy on the Other Side, but their experiences on this side help define who they are and how they may change after they cross over. What we go through here in the physical world helps shape the lessons of the soul, both here and on the Other Side.

For example, let's say that a white man was a bigot in his Earthly life and his daughter fell in love with and married an African-American man, causing a rift between father and child.

When this man dies and does his life review—that is, empties his pockets—I believe he'll find a pocket of judgment and prejudice and recognize that he allowed those beliefs in life to affect the relationship he had with his daughter. He'll then see the error in his old way of thinking.

People continue to learn and grow on the Other Side, and their growth may alter their energies. Hitler, for example, probably had to do a heavy-duty soul cleansing and life review as a result of the life he led here. Faced with his past, he might have seen his errors, understood them, and then tried to atone for them—perhaps by assisting others on Earth as a guide.

And there are no red-velvet ropes, VIP sections, or celebrities on the Other Side the way we define them here. Just because someone was famous in this life doesn't mean they're well known after they cross over. I believe that we only get "special treatment" once we cross over if we lived a truly good and spiritual life on the Earth plane—and if we truly absorbed the lessons we set out to learn. If we get far in our spiritual development here, we arrive there on more of an "advanced" level. Not that we're treated any differently, but we probably have less work to do and a lot more fun. But even though celebrities aren't signing autographs up *there*, they can still come through in readings and talk about signing autographs *here* . . . and explain who they were in this life.

In *CROSSING OVER: The Stories Behind the Stories*, I introduced you to Debbie Swift, the daughter of songwriter/singer Carl "Blue Suede Shoes" Perkins. Perkins's career was awe-inspiring, and he was truly a granddaddy of rock 'n' roll. However, when he came through to his family in a phone reading, he was just "Daddy," and not the famous person others perceive him to be.

The only clues I kept getting during the reading that made me think that the person coming through was famous in life were specific, celebrity-related items he was showing me. He showed me Elvis Presley's belt, and I saw images of celebrities such as Wynonna Judd, George Harrison, and Roy Orbison. At first, I thought I was just getting information in my usual, pop-culture way, until his daughter started acknowledging the celebrity names I was listing as the people who had been at her father's memorial or had worked with him in some way. That, I must say, was a wild experience.

I did another celebrity reading on *Crossing Over* the TV show where I read actress Tracy Nelson, the daughter of '50s teen heart-throb Rick Nelson. The reading was scheduled by the show's producers, who were careful to keep Tracy's identity a secret from me. To take the secrecy a step further, I arranged for her to sit down behind me after I was already sitting in the chair so that I couldn't see her face during the reading. I didn't do this to create any dramatic TV *oooohs* and *aaahhhhs*, but rather the opposite. I thought if I didn't see the person I was reading, whoever it was would relax during the session and pay closer attention to what I was saying without wondering if I'd recognized them and if I was giving them certain pieces of information because I recognized them.

I told Tracy to just respond with a yes or no, and the session began. Her dad came through almost immediately, and as soon as he did, he acknowledged that his sons were there in the studio as well, so the producers brought Ricky's twin boys, Gunnar and Matthew, to the stage to experience the session with Tracy. Now I had three celebrities sitting behind me, and one on the Other Side. But of the many validations that came through during that reading, there was only one detail I recall about him being famous—a reference to a performance he'd given at a theater like Carnegie Hall. That was it. From my perspective, the man coming through was basically a dad talking about his family and their personal, intimate connections with each other. The message that came through the strongest, which helped the family know that it was Dad, had nothing to do with his career accomplishments—rather, it was a reference to a special "coin" in the family. And one of the kids had brought the coin to the studio that day and had it in his pocket.

Another more recent example was one that will stick in my mind for years to come.

On a cold Thursday afternoon in February 2003, I was maneuvering through Manhattan traffic to get to a hotel on the west side for a reading I was asked to do. When working on my nonfiction books, I collaborate with another writer to make sure there's a journalistic objectivity to the readings we write about—whether they're transcribed directly or paraphrased from either my perspective or the perspective of the sitter. And in the case of any celebrity-related readings, I get the writer—in this instance, my friend and *People* magazine correspondent Natasha Stoynoff—to organize the session so I don't know whom I'm reading beforehand or any details about them.

This day, all I knew was that I'd be meeting with a client at 4 P.M. at a hotel in Manhattan's Columbus Circle area, at the foot of Central Park. I left early from my home in Long Island and drove into Manhattan, listening to my all-time favorite singer in the world, the amazing Linda Eder (I mentioned her earlier). Her latest CD, titled *Broadway, My Way* was in the CD changer, and I played it during the whole ride in. Linda's voice is so powerful that I listen to her music before most of my readings or events, and after them as well.

As she was belting out a ballad, Sandra called me on my cell phone. "Hey, where are you?" she asked. "Do you have a meeting today?"

"I'm on the Triboro Bridge on my way to do a reading Natasha scheduled for the book."

"Cooool . . . is it someone famous?"

"I have no idea. But I'll find out shortly. . . . "

AFTER I MADE IT INTO THE CITY, I had to maneuver through cars double-parked on both sides of 9th Avenue. An enormous snowstorm had hit the northeast three days earlier, and the piled-up snow made traffic even worse than usual in midtown Manhattan. I made it to my appointment right on time. Natasha, whom you'll read about throughout this book, met me in the lobby. She was there to tape-record and take notes on the session.

As we rode the elevator to the seventh floor, I looked over at Natasha, who was excited and nervous. Since she and I had begun working on this project, she had sat through more group readings and seminars than most people I know, and now this was to be her first, in-person private session to witness and document. We rang the bell of Suite 722, and a very attractive woman named Diane, whom I didn't recognize, answered the door and welcomed us in. She seemed very gentle, quiet, and sad.

We sat on the couch in front of a table laid out with a single red rose and a lit candle, and began what proceeded to be a very emotional, tear-filled session. Almost immediately, a strong energy took over and dominated the entire reading—which is rare. Usually three or four energies will come through in a private session, vying for attention.

Although you might be able to figure it out earlier than I did, it wasn't until we were finished over an hour later did I learn who the "celebrity" in question was. What follows is an abridged version of the reading, which is too long to include in its entirety. But I present most of it, in chronological order, so you can experience the process as it unfolded. And as you'll see, the information flowed with intensity—with messages from a strong energy who had a strong presence in life, too.

John: Okay, the first thing I'm going to tell you is that I have a male who's coming through, claiming to be above you, and he's making it like he's either your father or your stepfather, but he's an older male. He's making me feel that I need to acknowledge the letter "W," like he's connected to the letter "W."

I also have somebody younger who's passed. I feel like somebody lost their child. And the older man is letting me know that *the child is here.* But with this child, this isn't a health-care passing—this is something that happened.

So it's got to be an event or something that actually takes place that causes the person to pass. To me it feels impact related. So I feel like somebody passes with an impact, somebody passes with a vehicle accident, somebody passes with a gunshot, there's a BANG that takes place, and it's not a suicide. This is not a suicide, this is not somebody claiming responsibility—well, it's not that they're not claiming responsibility, they *are* kind of claiming responsibility.

They're making me feel like they put themselves in the wrong position, the wrong place at the wrong time.

And this event was extremely publicized. There are headlines and spotlights all around it. And they're showing me that there are three or four occurrences when people were reporting something that seems to be slightly off, like something was being reported and things were being left out of the report. And the way it was being reported made this individual look bad, and I feel as if I need to bring this up in some way. I don't know, it's like this weird—I don't want to call it controversy, but there's some controversial issue that comes up with this, okay?

Now, I'm going to go back and say that this male who's coming through again is claiming to be above you—that means the father, the uncle, the grandfather. He's telling me to let you know that he's here. He wants me to know that this younger male is coming through with him. I'm calling it a male energy because there's a very dominant energy attached to this. It may be female, but if this is a girl who's passed, I'm getting a very dominant energy. I have to let you know that he comes through with this child, but in particular, I know that you lost a child. You understand that? Is that true?

Diane: Yes.

John: Now there's an "A" name connection that comes up here. They want me to acknowledge the "A," okay? And they're making me feel like I also need to acknowledge the other son, the brother. They tell me to acknowledge the boy who's here.

They're showing me your son—living, then you have a daughter that passed. Right?

Diane: Yes.

John: Okay, here's the deal. She has a very dominant energy. The way it comes across, I would think you lost a son, because this energy is very masculine, very strong and tough. But her toughness is not exterior; it's not an external toughness. It's an internal, spiritual kind of toughness.

And she wants her brother to know that she came through. Her major concern is for you. She's making me feel like you two were more like sisters, or buddies. She wants me to tell you to talk about going to the church, going to the priest, going to the place, and you were there by yourself. I'm feeling a very spiritual-feeling place, whether it be a church, a temple, I don't know. I'm in this place, and while I'm here, I feel like nobody is physically there with you, it's like your quiet time, it's your place to be there. And she's making me feel like she was there with you.

I don't know if you're coming up on the second month of her passing, if you're coming up on the second anniversary of her passing, but I feel like we're coming up on two, and she's making me feel like I need to talk about you selling your property, or you selling the house, or you selling the stuff that's coming up, and she sees this. Okay? She doesn't talk about her father, though. The father is not around?

Diane: He is, he's around.

John: He's living?

Diane: Yes.

John: Where does the "L" come in for him? Like Len, or Leo or Lee or Leah . . . ?

Diane: That's her name.

John: She wants me to acknowledge the Len, Lee, Leo kind of version. I feel like—I want to take that and call her that . . . or Dad maybe called her that.

Diane: He called her LiLi most of the time!

John: She's telling me to tell you that what you wrote was published, that something you wrote was published, and she's acknowledging that. And she wants to know about the yellow tattoo or a yellow painting thing that comes up here that she wants me to bring up. Okay? She shows that.

I'm back to the fact that her passing was an event. There's an accident. But she's not driving this car; this is not something she was responsible for. But I feel like "I don't

31

have to be here," like "I don't have to be in the vehicle," like "I didn't have to be here."

Diane: Mm-hmm.

John: But it's the right time because she was done with what she had to do here, as hard as that might be to say. But I feel like she's doing more now there. She wants me to go back again, because one of the major things you're having a hard time with is how she passes.

Diane: Yes.

John: And she's making me feel like she doesn't want to tell me. She doesn't want to tell me how she passed. She's making me feel like you understand what I'm saying and I don't have to describe to you exactly what happened, although I'd rather hear it from her. But she's saying she won't, she's not going to go there.

She's making me feel like . . . she's in the backseat, and I feel like she could have been taking a nap, she could have had her headphones on, she could have been reading a book, whatever. There's all this hustle and bustle happening. She's getting whooshed off, like I feel like I'm being whooshed, like I have to go to my next place.

Diane (nodding): Yes . . .

John: Now, she did not pass on September 11th, but she's telling me to tell you 9/11, she's showing me 9/11. There's something about 9/11 connected to her in some way or to your family or to her, but it's like some of the families that I dealt with that are 9/11 related, they didn't have the ability to physically memorialize the person. You were able to do that in some respects, but there are things of hers that were not reclaimed, were missing, were things that you didn't get back.

Diane: Yes.

John: She's telling me that April is a significant month. It might be a birthday or an anniversary.

Diane: Okay . . .

John: Now, I feel very, very clearly that you walk around acknowledging her, you know there's something else. Your belief, your faith, and your spirituality are very much intact. What you're not honoring, and I'm sorry to put you on the spot, because I don't really know you, but what you're not honoring is your own grief. And one of the things that I have to tell you is that I believe the only way to get back the love that you have, that unconditional love as a parent for this child, is to honor that grief.

Because grief is the other side of love. When you take away the physical person, the object you direct that love toward, you don't know where to put that love. You don't know where it goes. But she's still here. She's still connected here. You know, she's the one who arranged this. It's like she's taking the credit for doing this. And she's making me feel that there's so much stuff left that's not finished with her, like the stuff that she was working on, something wasn't finished.

Diane: Yes, yes.

John: Did she write? She must have been a writer, 'cause she had to do something that would be—they're making me feel that something important is coming out, like being published. There's a writing thing about her. I think they're making a movie of her, or on a smaller level maybe you're making a documentary of her? They're showing me Selena. You're not related to Selena, are you?

Diane: No.

John: Then she's got to be like Selena.

Diane: Uh-huh.

John: She wants me to acknowledge your mom—your biological mom. Your mom and she have overlapping similarities. There's a parallel between both, whether it be the same names, similar dates, there's like a similarity that comes up there . . . and a few people pass in a short period of time as well . . . that you don't finish grieving one person and then this happens, that's my feeling. You're still dealing with the loss of one person, and now this compounds that feeling.

Diane: Yes.

John: If they're going to do something writing-wise about her, you need to do it. You need to be the person to do it. Not somebody else. With her own stuff, whatever she did job-wise, was she trying to get more active in the control?

Diane: Yes!

John: She wants you to learn the same. So when you do something, it's going to be therapeutic and healing to you, and you're going to get it right. Your son shouldn't do it—*you* should do it. Even if you have to work with a writer who's going to capture your voice, your feelings, and your private moments that you want to share. And then, if there's a movie or whatever, it can be made from your book. Not on what somebody else's idea is, or what they think it should be.

You know, I feel like—I don't know if that gold chain is yours, if she gave that to you, but she wants me to acknowledge that . . .

Diane: [crying]

John: She was very happy to help you accomplish things, to take care of you in some way. She wanted to make sure that stuff you did was in style and classy. It's all about classy. Everything's gotta be classy.

Diane: [nodding]

John: She's talking about getting hair, getting a wig. Is somebody going for hair extensions? Did somebody get some type of . . . after she passed, did you find something or have something delivered that was hers, hair related?

Diane: Yes.

John: From when she was a child?

Diane: Yes.

John: She must have been out of my state when she passed. She wasn't here in New York?

Diane: No.

John: Where's Betty? Betsy or Beebee, or there's a "B" name she's trying to acknowledge. It might be her way of saying hello to somebody who's still here. She said it's weird that you got this room. Was there something in this room when you got here that struck you as a sign from her? Or the number? What room is this?

Diane: 722.

John: 722? Does 722 have a meaning for you? This is a big building, and there could have been a lot of rooms they could have given you. But we got this one. She's highlighting this.

Diane: She was 22 when she passed.

John: Okay.

Diane: And she loved this hotel . . . it was her favorite.

John: You have an unconditional type of connection to her, that whatever she did you encouraged and were excited about. She doesn't want to tell me how she passed? I'm *begging* her . . . sometimes they won't do that; sometimes they feel like it's more important—and she does in this case—to move away from the physical passing and focus more on the living, on herself, on those still here. Did you make your own DVD or CD of her stuff, that other people wouldn't have access to?

Diane: I have a CD that only I have.

John: Nobody else has it, right? She's acknowledging that.

Do you have an SUV? She's telling me there's a joke about the navigation thing in the car—either her making a joke with you about that or you were driving and it was telling you where to go and telling you what to do, and you said out loud to yourself, or to her, that if she was here she'd be making fun of this.

Diane: Yes, she joked a lot about that!

John: She says something about the pink blouse, the pink shirt . . . do you still have that?

Diane: I do.

John: You just need to know that the stuff she's coming through with—the older man we talked about in the

beginning—that father figure, your mom, the great-aunt—
these are the people who are with her on the Other Side.
She's not alone; she's got family and friends there. She's very
clear in the fact that she was a social person in life, and she's
equally social on the Other Side.

Your spiritual beliefs—hold on to them. They're going
to pull you and your family through this. But she's making
me feel like you need to be the matriarch, that you need to
be the person that . . . you know when you sit on the
plane and the oxygen mask drops down and they say you
need to put your mask on first before you can help the person next to you? That's what your life is like right now. If
the mask drops down, you've got to make sure you take care
of yourself first. You've got to take care of *you* so that you
can be able to take care of the other people in your family.

Once you do that, then you can incorporate her still
being part of your life, and in *knowing* . . . and that word is
probably the one thing that I want you to leave here with
today: "knowing." Because the only thing that got me
through when I was 19 years old and just lost my mother
was that I had that *knowing.*

I remember pulling up one night at 5 A.M. after being
out all night and thinking, *Nobody cares right now that I'm
out at 5 A.M.* Sure, my grandmother was downstairs, and yes
she cared, but she was afraid to say anything to me.

My point in saying this right now is that I feel like
everybody's in that spot I just described. They're all pulling
up at 5 A.M. thinking that nobody else cares. Your son,
you, your husband. But every time you talk about your
daughter, you'll realize that you all care, you all care about
the same thing, and by honoring that and by talking about
her and what she's left . . . because according to her, she's
left a lot—and I don't mean money, I mean like her persona,
herself, her image . . . whatever. By honoring that, you can
know she's still connected by the bonds of love that bound
you all when she was here.

Diane: [crying softly now]

John: Okay, now she keeps showing me some sort of—I haven't said this yet because I don't know what it means, but she keeps showing me the parking garage on West 56th Street where I taped the show for the first two years. She's showing me standing at the entrance of that parking garage at West 56th. Do you have any ties to that parking garage on West 56th?

Diane: No.

John: I literally feel like I'm standing right there where there's the wall with the advertisements. I'm not sure if she's talking about the advertisements, could be, I don't know.

Diane: She used to go to the studio around there.

John: Maybe she parked there?

Diane: Could be . . .

John: But I need to make sure that you know that she's okay. And that she understands how painful of an experience today has been, and how painful dealing with all of this has been for you. And she's making me feel like it's really important that you know she appreciates everything you tried to do and that you continue to do. And she has let you know she's around. You do sense her, but at the same time you wish it away or you're kinda . . . "I'm making it up" or "I'm not really sure." Today's different, because it's like she's really unleashing herself on you in a way that you weren't ready for until very recently. And I feel like all of a sudden it became, "Okay, I can do this, I can do this."

Diane: Yes.

John: And then there's like an apprehension. I would have to say that within an hour before we even got here, you probably were saying, "I don't want to do this, I don't want to do this, I don't want to do this." Do you understand?

Diane: Yes, I do.

John: But she's okay. She's definitely, *definitely*, okay. Now when all this is said and done, I want you to have something tangible. And that little flower on the table, I don't think it's there by accident. So what I would like you to do is take that today, and that rose represents this experience. Because you need to have something tangible that we met, that she came through. This is very, very, important that she knows you have that. That's important for her.

Did she go by three names? Don't say the names, but did she go by three names?

Diane: Yes.

John: You know, just because somebody is physically not here, that doesn't mean we don't get the opportunity to work through some of the issues you didn't work through when they were here. So if you need to sit down and write a letter to your mom or write a letter to your aunt or write a letter to your daughter—any one of the people who have passed—to express and get out what you've been holding in for such a long time—it's not a bad thing.

One thing you need to realize is that if you were driving by yourself in a vehicle that maybe she never saw, and yet she can come here and talk about the fact that you have it and she sees you driving it and the fact that you were joking about the directions and what she would say if she was here, that's their way of continuing to let us know they're still connected to us. Those are the trivial, minute little details that validate the fact that they're still part of our lives. They do still see what's happening with us.

Let's say your daughter was still alive, and there was a different type of death—the death of the English language, and your daughter was only able to speak in ancient Aramaic, what would you do?

Diane: I'd learn the language.

John: Absolutely, you'd learn the language. That's how I want you to perceive this. Because she's still here, she's still connected to you. There's a different type of communication that's happening. It's the language of energy, and I do believe that she'll send you little signs, and she'll send you acknowledgments, and you might have a dream of her, you might have a feeling of her. But it's not something you should look for, because if you look for it, then you miss it. If it happens and you recognize it, that's a beautiful thing. If it happens and you're uncertain about it, acknowledge it in your mind: "Hey, I know you're here, I know you're trying, and thank you and keep up the good work. I appreciate it."

Diane: Does she know how much her friends love her? They miss her so much.

John: Absolutely. One of the major things people always say during a session is: "Tell her that I love her." My answer to that is: "You just did." You don't need to see a medium to connect with your daughter. Because the relationship is 365 days a year—and one day when the right time happens, you guys will connect again.

And when it's time for you to leave and you're done teaching and learning the lessons you need to learn here and you make that transition, I'm positive that the people we love will be there to meet you. Positive! I have no doubt! I know it from doing this work. People come through and say, "I was met by so-and-so," or "I was met by this one," or "I'm with these people."

I hope this has helped you. I can still feel the very emotionally charged situation in connection with her. Just know she's okay, and you and your son will be okay, too.

The energy pulled back, and I sat back in my chair, both tired and curious. Who was this celebrity? "I'm freaking out here," I said to Natasha and Diane. "You're going to tell me who this person is now . . . *right?!*

"John," said Natasha, "it's the young, beautiful, and talented *Aaliyah*."

Singer/actress Aaliyah had died in a plane crash on August 27, 2001, along with a group of friends and co-workers, when taking off in a small plane in the Bahamas. She was en route to New York after shooting a music video in the islands. Now it made perfect sense why she refused to tell me *how* she had died—not only would it have given me a major clue as to who she was, which could have made my knowledge "shut down" (I would have been self-conscious throughout the reading and would have known too much information from the get-go), but also, I was getting on a plane early the next morning and I hate—I mean *hate*—to fly. Natasha most likely didn't tell me so I wouldn't freak out and get nervous.

Once I knew who Diane's daughter was, other pieces of the puzzle started to come together, and I realized that this reading was indirectly connected to my publicist, Jill. A year and a half earlier, when it came time for me to pick someone to handle publicity after *Crossing Over* gained recognition, I chose Jill for a number of reasons. First, she'd been to the studio several times with other celebrity clients who had come for a reading, and I was impressed with how she looked after their interests and how kind yet super professional she always was. But after we'd had an official meeting together to see if we wanted to work together, I knew that there was another reason why I'd chosen her.

I told our supervising producer, Liz Arias; and Carol, my assistant, that I felt Jill *needed* to be connected to this work at this point in time—that it would help her. I wasn't sure what the reason was, and I didn't understand why I felt that way, but now I thought I knew the answer.

Jill and I were leaving the *Crossing Over* studio to do our first satellite TV interview one day, and on the way out of the building she told me that one of her clients had just passed—Aaliyah. That must have been what I was feeling when I first met her—that she was going to be questioning life and death, her own mortality, and grieving the death of someone close to her. That person must have been her close friend Aaliyah.

When Jill first told me about Aaliyah, I offered to talk to the singer's family, but it wasn't until now, a year and a half later, that Diane felt she was finally ready. I've often said that it's usually best for people to get through the initial stages of grieving before they consult with any medium. Mediumship should never be a first option, because what if the person you want to connect with doesn't show up? The trauma could exacerbate your grief.

Up until Natasha and I had arrived at the hotel, Diane was questioning her decision to get a reading— a fact that came through in the session. As she explained to me afterward, "I was in the hotel, and I walked around by myself thinking, *Should I do this? Does LiLi want me to do this?* I knew she had a very strong belief in the afterlife. She had begun to talk about it quite a bit as she got older, and she had bought books on it. That's another reason why I wanted to do it, because she had the belief. And the reading really did help me. It really did. It was amazing . . . there were so many parts that were so right on point. Some of the things you said were things that were so Aaliyah." Or "LiLi," as she was often lovingly called by her family. "She really was called three names: 'Baby Girl,' 'LiLi,' and then 'Aaliyah,'" said Diane, as she pointed out the validations in the reading.

As soon as the "dominant" energy came through to me, even though I thought it might be male, Diane knew it was her LiLi. "That was so on point," she says, "because she was sweet, thoughtful, compassionate . . . but at the same time, she had this strength that I was in awe of. I used to tell her, 'I think you are a magnificent human being, and I am truly in awe of you.' And she'd say, 'Really, Mom?'

"When something went wrong, she exhibited a strength that was magnificent. And I truly looked up to her." The two of them were indeed good buddies. "There was nothing she couldn't say to me and nothing I couldn't say to her," Diane remarked. "We talked about everything. She was my best friend. I would call her for advice! Who would think that a 22-year-old could give me advice! But that's how she was."

What really hit home for Diane were the little, intimate details that came through that only people close to her knew about. Like Aaliyah's pink clothes.

"The color pink, that was a color she began to like when she was about 18 years old. It was my mother's favorite color, and they were very close. All of a sudden one day, I noticed she'd been wearing a lot of pink . . . and I said, 'LiLi, you're liking pink now?' And she said, 'I don't know what it is . . . maybe it's Grandma!' Nobody really knew about this . . . maybe a couple of her close friends. For you to mention pink, it just hit me."

Other private moments, such as Diane's lone visit to their favorite church, also hit home.

"Aaliyah and I used to go to St. Patrick's Cathedral when we'd go shopping in the city. We'd be holding hands and we'd stop in there. A month after this happened, I went back to St. Patrick's alone, and I saw the priest and sat in on a service. I was by myself, trying to get some inner peace. And I've been there several times since."

Diane also confirmed that she has a piece of music of Aaliyah's that no one else has. "She made an audition CD to get into the performing arts high school, and she sang 'Ave Maria' in Latin. I found that CD, and we played it at the memorial mass we did for her. That CD is mine. No record company or anybody has it . . . it's mine, and it's awesome. It's just her with a piano accompaniment."

A reference that the family had written something about Aaliyah that was recently published was also true— "That was correct, too," acknowledged Diane. "Rashad wrote an article on his sister for *Teen Vogue* called 'Little Sister Lost' for the June 2002 issue."

One word that came up a few times in the reading was *classy*, which Diane says describes her beautiful daughter to a T.

"She always wanted to do things in a 'classy' way," said Diane. "And that was always how we described her. And when you said she was the kind who lived without regrets, that was so true, too. She would always say, 'You know . . . you can't live your life like that . . . ya gotta do what you gotta do . . . what will be, will be.' So when you said that, it was almost like she was talking to me right there in the room. LiLi liked to live in the moment, and whatever that moment was, she cherished it, she embraced it, and she always said, 'We have no control. If something's going to happen, it's going to happen.'"

As Diane and I continued to talk after the reading, some other validations started to emerge. I realized that the parking-lot reference was a validation directed toward *me*—I had parked in that lot every day when I was working at the studio nearby and remembered that there was a gigantic billboard for the movie *Queen of the Damned,* with Aaliyah's face about 20 feet high next to the lot. I couldn't help but see that billboard each day for months as I entered the studio. Diane also made the connection for the male with the "W" name who appeared first in the reading, bringing through her daughter.

"My best friend, Keeth Wallace, he was on the plane with Aaliyah. I didn't get it at first. He was very close to us, and like an uncle to LiLi. That's why he went with her on this trip. Because I had surgery and couldn't go, he took days off from work to go with her. He said, 'Diane, since you can't go, I'll go.'"

As our session came to a close, Aaliyah's strong energy still lingered in the room. I saw a flash of an ethnic-looking bracelet in my mind's eye.

"Diane," I asked, "where's the bracelet? Do you know if she had a scarab—an Egyptian bracelet?"

Diane wasn't sure, although she did know that her daughter had a lot of Egyptian jewelry. Diane's homework was to check on the bracelet as well as other information she didn't understand—such as the "B" name that I'd gotten. [Diane now believes that this might be her niece, Blair, whose birthday is in April—this would refer back to April being significant, and the "B" name.]

Although Diane's spirits seemed a little lighter than when we'd first shaken hands an hour earlier, I could still feel the high emotion of the loss for her.

"Sometimes it's all so unbearable," she said, softly weeping. "Some days, I just want to . . . I'm in a daze. Yesterday I just walked in circles and cried my heart out. It's hard to go on. . . . "

"That's a very human feeling," I told her, "but you're still here because you've got stuff you need to do. You have to be the person to honor your daughter's memory. Because then people are really going to get a chance to understand who she is."

Before I departed the hotel—with Diane clutching the red rose as a memento—I left her with one last thought. "Diane, I want to be bold enough to tell you this: Your daughter is larger than a plane crash. That plane crash happened in a minute, but her life was a lot longer than that. You have to look at everything she accomplished. And even though she did leave us physically, she's still here; she's still connected to you. And the love you have for her and the love she has for you is still very much here and alive."

I reminded Diane that the most important thing for her to do now was to honor her grief—to feel the pain so she could get back to feeling some joy instead of pacing around her apartment and cutting herself off from life.

"Aaliyah is still connected to you, and she's counting on you," I told her. And all of us must remember this when we lose someone we love. Cry, then pick yourself up bravely, because they're watching over us and hoping we'll do well during the rest of our years here, fulfilling whatever destiny we have.

"And one day you will see her again," I told her. "I promise you . . . one day, when the time is right, you will see your daughter again."

CHAPTER THREE

Going Down Under

A ROO IN THE HEADLIGHTS

UNTIL I STEPPED FOOT ON RUGGED AUSSIE TERRAIN, I always thought that a wombat was one of those mythical creatures, like a unicorn or a mermaid. I never thought I'd one day be holding one—never mind doing a *psychic reading* on one.

I'd arrived in Sydney, Australia, the day before to embark on a two-week seminar tour in January 2003—the first one I'd done outside of the United States since I began this work. In the last few years, I've had countless invitations to conduct seminars in other countries including England, Canada, and even Japan—where I was offered $100,000 (U.S.) to do two one-hour TV appearances—but I always turned them down. Why? First and foremost, I'm not motivated by money, and I know that the green stuff can never be the force behind spiritual work like this. If it is, then my work will inevitably suffer.

I know that a lot of people don't believe me when I say this, because they see me as a TV celebrity "cashing in" with books and seminars and such. But I stand by my words: I honor the work and the process first. The other reasons I turned down the invitations are that I'm naturally a homebody and don't like to travel too far from my family, and also—I'm quite patriotic. I always felt if I had the time and energy to do this work, I should do it for my own country. And, God knows, it wasn't as if I were running out of dead people here. But after *Crossing Over* went into syndication in Australia, the people "down under" really took to the subject matter, and the show took off like a rocket.

"Why don't you go down?" Reid Tracy, president of Hay House, Inc. (the distributor of this book), urged me over lunch one day last spring. "The show is a hit, and the people love you. It would be fun, like a vacation. Go somewhere new. Take the family. . . . "

Carol, my assistant, was lunching with us and began to launch into our standard excuse about how I don't like to leave the country . . . blah, blah, blah. So I don't know what came over me, but in a moment of inspiration, I interrupted Carol's speech with an *"Okay, let's do it!"* Carol and Reid were shocked—Reid *pleasantly* so, since he thought he'd have to do way more convincing than that. But I was probably more stunned than either of them. Reid was right—maybe it *was* time to spread my wings and have a bit of an adventure.

Before I could change my mind, he had arranged a two-week, three-city tour, and when tickets went on sale, they sold out in a record nine minutes for venues holding up to 10,000 people. So far the biggest group I'd ever worked with was an audience of 8,000 in Anaheim, California—but that time I was one of four speakers. This time it was going to be just me, *solamente*.

I had no worries about getting the job done—there could be 50,000 people in a room and someone might be sitting in the last row in a dark corner . . . but if I'm meant to read them, I'll feel the pull and find them. So I wasn't worried about the Other Side speaking up loud and clear. I was more worried about us *living* beings on *this* side understanding each other. Would the rugby player in Brisbane be able to comprehend my obscure American pop-culture references? Would I understand *their* lingo? And then there was the accent. When I was visiting the Dominican Republic with a friend over a decade ago, I tried to show off my limited understanding of Spanish by conversing with a waiter. The only thing was, I had to ask him to repeat what he was saying three times, and *slower,* please—until my buddy Lisa couldn't stand it anymore.

"He wants to know if you want a glass of water!" she blurted out.

"How do you know that?" I asked.

"John . . . he was speaking *English!*"

But in Australia, the communication gap started before I even got there. During a stopover in Los Angeles, I gave a satellite interview with the Australian version of the *Today* show. The reporter started out with the usual questions: "When did you know you were psychic? How does it work?" And then she hit me with a zinger. "John," she continued, leaning in,"what would you say to one cynic here in Australia who says you're just an elitist vulture circling the corpses?"

Ouch. I couldn't believe this woman had just asked me that. I'm all for somebody expressing their views and saying they don't believe in what I do . . . but have a little respect, please. (I don't even remember how I answered her, as I'd slept very little that night and felt groggy and edgy.)

Boarding the flight for Sydney, everything was in slow motion— my thoughts, my reactions, even the rapid-fire speech that I'm so infamous for (and often admonished for)—and I wondered if my guides were "slowing me down" to make sure that not only would I understand my foreign audience, but they'd understand *me.* By the time we reached the customs counter in Sydney 20 hours later, my reflexes were set on "sluggish."

"What's in the tins?" the customs guy asked as he ruffled through my luggage.

"Excuse me?" I had no idea what he was talking about.

"What's in the *tins,* mate? *The tins!*" My friend Jesse, who was behind me in line, pointed to my six-pack of protein drinks as I watched the customs guy shake them and read the tiny ingredients list on the back. Once he was confident I wasn't bringing in any strange American animal product into the country, he waved me on.

We arrived at our hotel in downtown Sydney for one night's rest before traveling to Brisbane, where the seminars were slated to start. As soon as I checked in, I took a much-needed walk around the edge of the harbor by the Sydney Opera House to stretch my legs after that long flight. To tell you the truth, my first glimpse of Sydney reminded me of downtown Manhattan. From where I stood, I imagined looking to my right and seeing the Statue of Liberty. I telephoned Sandra in New York and woke her up.

"What time is it over there?" she asked, half-asleep.

"I have a better question for you," I responded. "What *day* is it?" I had crossed the international dateline and was 16 hours ahead of home time. My body clock was in flux. I'd traveled into the future.

Sandra and Justin had stayed home on this trip since he was barely four months old and we thought it best he stay landlocked for a few more months. Accompanying me instead was a group of friends and co-workers: *Crossing Over* executive producer Paul Shavelson, producer/cameraman Duncan Cameron, and actor and camera dude Jesse Shafer (all there to shoot a documentary about the tour for the Travel Channel); my buddy and *TV Guide* reporter Michael Logan; my publicist, Jill, and her boyfriend, Jack Rico—a journalist for the Spanish TV station Univision; and Natasha (the *People* magazine correspondent I introduced you to earlier), my collaborator on this book.

After another sleepless night on my part, we all hopped into a water taxi the next morning and headed off to our first tourist attraction—The Taranga Zoo. And this is how it came to be that I "read" a wombat. As soon as we arrived at the zoo, a tour guide plopped little Digby, a baby wombat, into my arms. He was really cute and lovable, even if he did look kind of like a humongous rat. The guide filled me in on the wombat's tragic history and told me that his mother had been hit by a car months before and he had been found in the pouch, alive, and had been brought to the zoo to live. As she was talking, I started to pick up on Digby's energy.

"Did he have a problem with his skin or his fur when he first came in?" I asked. Yes, he did, she said. Before I knew it, I was spouting out all sorts of information, casually, as if I read wombats every day. Reid Tracy, who was also with us that day, was the first one to notice. "Oh my God," he exclaimed, "he's reading the wombat!"

Well, to be more specific, I was getting information from my guides *about* the wombat. It's not like I was getting Digby's mother coming through . . . or a wombat *to his side*. But I think anybody who has pets knows what it's like to connect with an animal psychically. I'm always able to sense when our dogs, Jolie and Roxie, are hungry before they come to me with their tongues hanging out of their mouths. Digby would be the first of many animals I would connect with on this trip . . . you might say he was my "warm-up" wombat.

At the zoo, I also got a taste of my apparent "celebrity status" in Australia. Probably ten times more people than usual recognized me with a nod or a smile, but it was much more relaxed than what happens in the States. They didn't come up to me and demand a reading on the spot like some New Yorkers do on Manhattan sidewalks. One little boy about seven years old approached me and asked if I would pose in a picture with him and his school chums, all big fans of the show. Well, that just about blew my mind. I was amazed that *Crossing Over* was reaching such a young audience here and could only assume that there must be more of an openness toward spirituality in general in this country. My theory would prove to be right.

Leaving the zoo that day, I had a moment of homesickness . . . and felt a warm, powerful sense of my mother around me, embracing me like a warm sweater. I was standing next to this big glass tank filled with sea lions, and I looked into the water. Two seconds later, a white feather started to slowly float upward in the tank.

"Duncan, *get that on tape!*" I said as I grabbed our camera guy. Duncan began to roll film, all the while asking me why he was shooting a boring tank of water. What did it mean? That's a job hazard (or perk, depending on how you look at it) when you work with me—most things usually mean *something*.

"It's a message from an old friend," was all I told him, and a second later the tape ran out.

As some of you might know, the feather was a message from my mom. In my second book, *CROSSING OVER: The Stories Behind the*

Stories, I revealed the three signs my mother and I decided upon together before she died that she'd send me from the Other Side (a reference to her nickname, "Princess"; a reference to Pooh Bear; and some mention of the town Springfield from her favorite soap, *Guiding Light*). But right after she passed, I also asked her to send me one additional sign to let me know she was making the transition okay—and that sign was a white bird. That white bird appeared on a floral arrangement at her funeral, giving me the validation I needed. Since then I've received the "abridged" version— a white feather—several times, and that, too, has come to mean a message from my mom. There I was, thousands of miles from home and already feeling homesick, and here was Mom to remind me: *You're not alone.*

By the time we reached Brisbane for the first two seminars, I was running on four days of no sleep and walked out onstage with my body and brain still on 4 A.M. Eastern Standard Time. But as soon as I keyed into the enthusiasm of the 4,000 people packed into the convention center that first night, their energy lit me up like a Christmas tree, and I was on. I was able to give dozens of mini-readings that night, which were simultaneously projected onto three giant screens in the venue for everyone to watch. In total, we did so many fantastic readings during the Australia tour that I could write a whole book on it. Here, I'll include just a few snippets.

In one of the early readings the second night, I was drawn to a woman in the front row as the sound of gunshots went off in my head.

> **John:** Somebody here was shot. Somebody passes from a gunshot in this area.
>
> **Woman:** My husband was shot.
>
> **John:** By somebody he knows? Because I have a familiar feeling attached to this—
>
> **Woman:** Yes. He was murdered by a friend of a friend.
>
> **John:** And the friend got away with it?
>
> **Woman:** He got away with it for a few hours.
>
> **John:** I have a feeling that . . . as far as being punished, it's like the person got off in some way.

Woman: Yes. The person who shot my husband was an escaped prisoner, and my husband's friend was harboring him. I don't think he meant for the prisoner to actually take the shot at my husband that killed him, but he was as much to blame as the other one, even though he wasn't the murderer.

John: He was your second husband. . . .

Woman: Yes.

John: Can I be really blunt?

Woman: I would expect that, actually.

John: Did you hit him?

Woman: Um, we hit each other. He was very frustrating . . . but I didn't hit him hard! [laughter in the room]

John: Let me tell you what he's showing me. He's making me feel like he provoked a level of emotion in you that would make you do that. Follow me?

Woman: Correct.

John: He asks if you're going to get your two back teeth pulled or fixed.

Woman (laughs): I haven't had time to do it yet!

John: But do you know what he means?

Woman: Yes!

The brief reading I did on this woman, whose name I later found out was Kerry Davies, shows how a loved one from the Other Side often picks out a small yet intimate detail to identify him- or herself to their relatives. In this case, Kerry's husband, Peter, brought up his wife's teeth that still needed to be fixed.

After the reading, Kerry, 44, a homemaker living outside of Brisbane, commented on her experience. "I couldn't believe that came through. Peter always used to say to me, 'You're a beautiful woman, but you have to get something done about your teeth!' because I'm losing them in the back. And that was quite funny to hear. No one else knew that."

But in his brief appearance, Peter also touched upon the serious issues of their volatile relationship and his murder. "Peter was quite violent because he had been a heroin addict for 20 years," Kerry explained. "But he had finally given it up. And it was sort of sad, because after he died, we got the medical report and it said he was clean. I couldn't believe it . . . because six months before he wasn't. Now he was, and he was dead."

His murder 15 months earlier had been big news in the local papers—an escaped convict harbored by a friend of Peter's killed him because he suspected Peter was going to turn him in to the police.

"I walked into the front yard and saw him shoot my husband with a 30-30, blowing his head off in front of me," Kerry described. "Peter was lying there . . . and I could feel the zapping of his energy. For three days afterwards, I knew he was in the house with me . . . I could feel it. It was a frantic energy, a frantic spirit. And then it just seemed to go. Although I still often feel Peter's energy in the house with me, I don't feel that frantic panic anymore."

As the evening progressed, I noticed that a lot of people, like Kerry, seemed to be in touch with their own psychic side or intuitive abilities. I asked Sydney-based Leon Nacson, managing director of Hay House Australia, about it. "It's cultural," he told me. "We're more apt to seek out self-empowerment, psychology, and self-help."

My own theory was also this: Since Australians are somewhat isolated from the rest of the world, and their country is less densely populated than many, they're more in touch with their primitive feelings and learn to rely on their instincts and intuition, so their spirituality has been fostered. That same night, I keyed into yet another high-profile murder case, this time involving a young girl, which was solved by one relative's psychic vision. It was a highly emotional reading for the two family members in attendance, but in the midst of all the seriousness, I also had a little laugh at myself as I stumbled across my first Australian-American pop-cultural gap. Did the Australians know who Howdy Doody was? I was about to find out.

John: I have a younger female coming through . . . a younger sister, a niece. I don't think it's a daughter. I'm with someone with a "Benny" sound . . . a Bonnie, Benny . . . a "B" name.

Woman: I have a step-granddaughter who was tragically killed.

John: She's not coming through as a daughter; she's coming through as a sister. . . .

Woman (pointing to young woman next to her): She was like a sister to my daughter.

John: She's coming through below you, so was she much younger than you?

Daughter: Yes.

John: I need to acknowledge she's here, and there's a unique "B" name connected to her.

Woman: Her last name was Beasley.

John: There's an unanswered feeling about this. There are question marks all over the place, as if you guys have not had the answers you would have liked. Do you understand this?

Woman: Yes.

John: I have an out-of-country feeling about this. The person who did this, was he not from here?

Woman: Right, he came from another country.

John: Now, I could be bringing in someone completely different here . . . but . . . was she strangled? She was either strangled or asphyxiated because I feel like I can't breathe.

Woman: Yes! She was asphyxiated. We have an idea how it happened, but we don't know all the details.

John: This is going to sound strange, but . . . it does feel like it was an accident to me.

Woman: He was saying that from the beginning . . . that he didn't really mean to do it . . . that it was an accident.

John: It was *not* intentional. I don't feel a brutal, intentional, premeditated feeling. This is a quirky, irresponsible event . . . but I'm not saying it was acceptable. She's show-ing me pink roses. She wants me to talk about the white bird connection you have. Did you have a special floral arrange-ment made for her?

Woman #2 (sitting next to her): Yes, my daughter did.

John: She wants me to acknowledge a special floral arrangement. *Special.* Not just flowers . . . there's also a thing about a white bird.

Woman #2: Yes, I had a special floral arrangement made.

John: She's got the cousin with her on the Other Side. The male figure to her side.

Woman: That would probably be her half-brother who passed as a baby.

John: Please let the family know she came through and that they need to let go of how she passed. They're too stuck on this. You're never going to forget it; it's never going to go away. But to find some type of closure and heal-ing, you need to move away from the event so you can move through your grief.

You have to go on that journey, because when you get through your grief, you get back to love. It's like grief is the other side of love.

Woman: Okay . . .

John: And she's making me feel like . . . do you know who Howdy Doody is? She's showing me Howdy Doody.

Woman: No . . .

John: Um . . . okay . . . uh . . . how do I describe this . . . he's a puppet . . . and . . . *red hair and freckles?!*

Woman: Oh, that's my other daughter, Harmony! She has red hair and freckles!

Young Sheree Beasley, only six years old, was riding her pink bike one sunny afternoon in 1991 when she was abducted and mur-dered. She was missing for three months before police found her dead in a drain under a country road, her clothing scattered at the scene, and her body so decomposed she had to be identified by her nails. Not only was the case big in the papers in Australia, but one of the detectives on the case wrote a book about the investigation called *The Murder of Sheree Beasley*. Sheree came through at the seminar for her step-grandmother, Denise Greenhill; and aunt, Adele, with details of her murder and the hopes that her family would move on from the horrible way she died.

"The guy who did it claimed the killing was accidental, that he never meant to do it, he never meant for it to go that far," Denise confirmed, "but that didn't lessen our anger toward him. We still feel the anger. How do you get over that?" After the police had found the body of a young girl, they had trouble identifying it, and the only item of clothing left on her was a T-shirt with a picture of a big cat on the front. Sheree's mother couldn't remember what her daughter had worn the day she was abducted because Sheree had dressed herself that morning—or if she even owned a T-shirt like that. But that night, Denise had a dream—of Sheree standing in front of her wearing her beloved roller skates . . . and a T-shirt with a cat on it. She got up and woke her husband, who then contacted Sheree's paternal grandparents. They rifled through the family photo albums and found a picture of Sheree wearing that same shirt.

Hearing Sheree come through at the seminar helped the family find some closure. Denise remarked, "Sheree must have known that we really needed to hear from her. We've all had such trouble dealing with her death and getting past how it happened. But she says we have to just get past it. I know we have to. I will take that message home with me—especially to my ex-husband—that we have to live on."

KARANGATUDE!

MY NEWFOUND KINSHIP WITH THE NATIVES—and I'm talking about the animal kingdom here—continued, to the point where Leon joked that he was going to nickname me "Dr. Doolittle." On yet another tourist adventure, our group packed into a bus like schoolkids and made our way to Steve Irwin's Australian Zoo—founded by Mr. Crocodile Hunter himself!

On the ride there, the landscape looked strangely like suburban Florida. The roads were lined with palm trees and strips malls, with Burger Kings and McDonald's—which was all very fine and good by me. I'm a lifelong picky eater, so by day five I was subsisting on the familiar: Mickey D's.

Jill, a fellow food purist, was living on chocolate and French fries but no burgers—after biting into one at the hotel, she became paranoid that they were made of kangaroo, or "roos," as we now called them, as per the local slang. As the landscape whizzed by, we passed a street named "Edward Street," and then a block later, a street named "Gallery on Edward." I took it as a sign that I was on the right road.

The first thing I noticed about the Australian Zoo was that, in a funny way, I felt as if the *humans* were the attraction. Usually when you go to a zoo, the animals are in cages and the people mill about staring at them. Here, you walk among the animals' natural habitats, and they come right up to you and check you out. We petted the dingos (and I had to hold myself back from doing my Meryl Streep impression: "A dingo stole my baby!"), fed the kangaroos, and took our turns doing "the koala cuddle," as they call it, balancing a little koala named Lawson on our chests. After lunch, I was feeling daring enough to let one of the guides wrap Rosie, a boa constrictor, around my neck. (She was named Rosie for her pink cheeks, I was told.) The whole place was very impressive, and I really feel that Steve Irwin is an amazing man doing incredible things to educate people about animals and to provide a good home for these wonderful creatures. If that doesn't come across in his TV shows, I'm telling you now—his dedication to their cause is admirable.

The energy of the animals at the zoo was so pure that I once again felt an easy and natural connection with them. But even I was a bit surprised when we met Harriet, a 178-year-old turtle who had at one time belonged to evolutionist Charles Darwin. As Harriet nibbled at the hibiscus flowers from my open palm, I started plugging into her energy. . . .

"Who's the blonde girl who used to look after Harriet?" I asked our guide.

"Oh, that's Joy! She used to take care of her."

"Did she talk differently than everyone else?"

"Yes, yes, she had a very strong English accent."

"Did you ever keep Harriet in a different part of the zoo? Because I'm getting that she likes it better here than where she used to be. She felt kind of isolated there."

"Yes! She used to be closer to the entrance; it was away from the people."

"Did someone knit her a special blanket? Did someone mark her on her back?"

The information kept coming, and the guide kept validating. And Reid, of course, was flipping out all over again. For the rest of the trip, I'd hear him on his cell phone time and again telling someone, "He read a freakin' wombat and a turtle!"

But Jill, a Manhattan publicist in the truest sense of the job description, was naturally pushing for more play here.

"John," she asked, as I was quietly communing with Harriet, "do you think you can get *Darwin* to come through . . . ?"

FROM BRISBANE, IT WAS BACK to Sydney for three seminars. I stepped onstage the first night in Sydney, and the applause was deafening. I actually got a standing ovation for just walking out there! It was staggering.

I'd been reading the local reviews of the seminars we'd done so far, and the critics were writing that I had "rock-star status" and that the people were "embracing" me. While I do appreciate acceptance like that, I don't want people to pay too much attention to the messenger and miss the message. It's not about me; I'm just the speaker . . . an amplification of the process. In the past, attention like that used to make me feel embarrassed and self-conscious, until I broke it down mentally in a way that made sense to me: The audiences aren't really clapping for me, but for their own relatives. The yells and cheers are for what I represent. They might think they're clapping for the guy on TV, but ultimately what they're applauding is the idea that their loved ones are still connected to them. And I would clap for that, too.

Oftentimes, I wish people at the seminars could see the bizarre pictures I'm shown when loved ones from the Other Side try to capture my attention. Let me just say this: The Other Side has one wacky sense of humor. I started off one night with an image in my mind of a woman biting her toenails with her teeth as she watched television. Was I seeing this correctly? Could this be right? You betcha. After much prodding on my part, the nail biter, a former contortionist, it turns out, eventually raised her hand and owned up to her nasty habit so she could get her messages from Mom on the Other Side.

There were no drinks and food allowed in the auditorium we were in, but that same night I got an image of a hunk of gooey cake someone was hiding in a purse. I could practically taste it.

"Who's got the cake?" I demanded. I got off the stage and walked through the aisle looking for this mystery dessert. Finally, one woman shyly raised her hand.

I pointed to her. "Show me the cake!" And voilà, she did—she produced a wedge of cake from her pocketbook. She had bought it on the way to the seminar because she'd missed dinner and had planned to secretly nibble on it throughout the evening. After she admitted to her "cake crime," then, and only then, could I give her the messages from her dad on the Other Side.

Sometimes the images I get start even before I arrive at an event, and at the most inopportune moments. It was our first workday in Sydney, about five hours before the seminar that night, and I was in the shower washing up after a gym workout. Just as I was rinsing the shampoo out of my eyes, I got a nudge from a boy on the Other Side.

"Hey," I urged him, "come back tonight when your relatives are in front of me!" I was eager to finish washing my hair . . . *alone*. He obliged. So when I got to the event later that evening, I started off the readings with David, the shower crasher.

John: At 1 P.M. this afternoon, someone's son came through to me while I was in the shower. He's coming through for his mom. He's been gone a long time, 20 to 30 years. He was there to meet Dad. Dad just passed. There's a February connection here. And the woman I'm looking for is white-haired or gray-haired or platinum blonde. The son needs to let the mom know not to worry about Dad. I'd like to know what you were doing at one o'clock this afternoon. And there's also a connection to the 16th.

Woman: My son died 20 years ago, but my husband died before him.

John: There's another male figure to the side there for you. February is important here. You must have the February connection.

Woman: I have a grandson who will be two years old in February.

John: This male figure showed up at 1 P.M. today, and he's the son, gone 20 years. He was there to connect to an older male figure after him, and he says you'd have another contemporary there as well, that you lost a male to the side as well. Is Richard connected to you? Or Robert? Who is the "R" name?

Woman: My husband is Robert.

John: And there is a train reference here.

Woman: My older brother worked with the railways for a long time.

John: Were there six of you? I'm getting you were a family of six kids.

Woman: I was one of five.

John: Do you know if your mom miscarried?

Woman: Oh, yes, she did . . . one time.

John: With your husband, Robert, was there a question of someone's paternity? Or that someone acted as a father to someone's child? Or maybe there's a joke about the paternity of a child. . . .

Woman: Yes, my husband's brother kind of took over for the kids as a father figure.

John: He helped with their schooling.

Woman: Yes.

John: There's a story about the man who acted as the father figure, a story about him being shot. But he did not die of this gunshot. He died the same way Robert and your son died, with an impact. They all died from something impact related.

Woman: Yes.

John: And someone is known for raising chickens or birds.

Woman: Yes, my brother raised birds!

Kay Dunn's son, David, had died in a car accident 20 years earlier, and Kay told us after the reading that she got the news of her son's death through a visit from her father in a dream.

"The day my son was killed, I woke up after having had a dream of my father sitting on a fence with all this green grass around him, and he was telling me, 'Don't worry, everything's going to be all right.' I remember looking at the clock when I woke up that morning, because I was a bit shook up, wondering, *Gee, what was that? Why did I have a dream like that?* A few hours later, [the authorities] came and told me that David had died, and it had happened just a little bit before the time I had the dream. I don't talk to people about this much because I think people will laugh at me!" Kay's son, her husband, and her brother-in-law all passed in vehicle accidents, she confirmed, which came through in the reading with the three "impact"-related deaths.

Kay's son also had a knack for unique timing like his grandfather when it came to coming through from the Other Side. At 1 P.M. that day, as David's energy ambushed me in the shower, Kay and her niece, Jan, were having lunch with friends and telling them about the seminar that night. "At about 1 P.M., I said, 'Look, we've got to go . . . we need to get ready because we're seeing John Edward tonight,'" Jan recalled.

The seminars in Sydney ended on a sentimental note when two brothers, separated by death, reunited using their love of a football (or soccer, to us Yanks) team as their means of connection. It was also one of many funny moments during the trip that made the audience chuckle at my self-confessed lack of macho sports knowledge.

> **John:** Someone has a dog on their shirt.
> **Man** (standing up): I do, it's the Bulldog.
> **John:** There's a bulldog on your shirt?
> **Man:** Right . . . from the football team. Best football team in the world!
> **John:** I'm sports-illiterate in the U.S., never mind Australia! Someone wants me to acknowledge your marriage, and they weren't able to be there physically, but they were at your wedding from the Other Side. And I need to acknowledge the two kids.
> **Man:** Yes, yes.
> **John:** They want me to talk about the man with the really strong, baritone-type voice.
> **Man:** We had an uncle who had a really loud voice like that.
> **John:** And they clearly want me to acknowledge the older male figure who was at the wedding.
> **Man:** I had an older brother
> **John:** He'd wear the same shirt as you?
> **Man:** Of course! We buried him in it.
> **John:** I was going to say . . . there's a joke about burying him in an opposing team's shirt! He says he would not be wearing that shirt. He says there was another team he liked a little bit more. . . . Who's Steven? He could be a player for all I know.
> **Man:** There was a player, Steven, who was a favorite when my brother was alive.
> **John:** Then I have to tell you, that team was a "different" team when he was alive.
> **Man:** No, it's not the same team now . . . all the players are different, and the shirt is different.
> **John:** Your brother sends a hug to Mom.
> **Man:** She's right here, next to me.

John: He says that when he passed, your mom said that he'd be illuminating heaven.

Mom: Yes, I say that all the time.

"As soon as you said there's a dog on a T-shirt," recalled Angelo Dimitrakas, "my wife was nudging me to get up, get up!" At the last minute before coming to the seminar, Angelo decided to put on his old football jersey belonging to the Canterbury Bulldogs, his favorite Sydney football team, when he and his older brother, who passed over in 1994, were growing up. They buried Angelo's brother in the jersey the team wore when he passed away.

"We joked a bit about swapping the shirt and putting him in another jersey," Angelo said. "If I'd done that, he would have really been ticked off. But it's true that when he was alive it was really a different team, a different generation, and a completely different jersey but with the same colors. Now the team has all new players. The other team was always on top, but this new team is way behind. So when he says it's a different team . . . it sure is."

Angelo's brother had died a few months before Angelo's wedding and before the birth of his two kids, which Angelo acknowledged in the reading, as well as noting the loud uncle with the booming voice: "That man, when he talked, not only did the whole room hear him, but the whole neighborhood heard him." And finally, "My brother was the life of the party, and he made an impression on everybody he met. When he died, we thought that he'd do the same there, in heaven. My mother says it all the time: 'He'll brighten the place up—up there.'"

BEFORE MOVING ONWARD TO MELBOURNE, there was one more journey to take. Everyone kept telling me I had to do "The Bridge Climb" in Sydney, but I had no idea what that was. Then, from the balcony of my hotel, I saw it: The long Sydney Bridge stretched out far and very high, with people who looked like tiny little ants making their way up it. *Hmm. I don't know about this.*

Because we were filming the *John Edward Goes to Australia* documentary, Paul had instructed Jesse and Duncan to film my every waking moment on this trip and get me doing something more interesting than ordering my daily Happy Meal at McDonald's. But if you know me, you know that I'm not exactly the easiest person to "capture." Even though I had agreed to do the documentary, I didn't want a camera stuck in my face all the time. In fact, I'm sure Duncan and Jesse have at least 50 censored bloopers from our two-week trek showing me holding my hand up to the lens, threatening their lives, or describing to them in detail just how painful a tripod up their . . . how do they say it in Australia?—their *backsides*—would be.

But Paul was excited to capture the whole climb on film and told me I had to do it for his art. He then informed me that he, of course, would *not* be accompanying me on the climb, as he was afraid of heights. Ah, this is where the fun began for me. If he wasn't coming, I told him, I wouldn't do it. So the whole gang—Paul, Jill, Jack, Mike, Duncan, Jesse, Natasha, and me—filed into the chamber where you register and go through "training" for the climb.

One wall was covered with photos of celebrities who had done the climb and lived to pose for a portrait, and I noticed that they were all wearing the same outfit—a sort of gray jumpsuit with a Batman-like utility belt. The belt, our trainer explained, would hook us onto a cable that lined the bridge the whole way up and down, so if a strong gust of wind knocked us over, we wouldn't plummet to our deaths. No. Instead, we'd just dangle there for a while until someone could hike over and rescue us. I glanced over at Paul, who had gone pale. He looked at me with an "Are you really going to make me do this?" look. Yep, I was.

Because our group was so big, Jack and Jill joined the group behind us (and please, no jokes about their names and the fact that they were about to go "up a hill" together—they've heard it all). What I didn't know was that Jill was also freaked out about making the climb. After we changed into our gear and watched the instructional video, it was time to march on.

Duncan and Jesse hooked me up for sound with a wireless microphone, and we followed our tour guide, a very pretty young woman named Amanda. We had a choice, she told us: We could either take the elevator to the top and then walk across the bridge only a short distance, *or* we could climb each of the rafters, level by level, over the Sydney harbor and across the fast-moving traffic below. Paul perked up at the first suggestion.

"Oh, no," I told Amanda, with a smile, "we want to do the whole climb, every step of it."

I have to share with you the pleasure I was getting in making Paul squirm. Paul and I have a great relationship, but because a good portion of it is spent on work-related stuff, it's usually about him making me do things I don't want to. For example, he'll make me record voice-overs for the show again and again until I get it just right because he heard a little something in the background. Or, when I introduce a segment—a "wraparound"—on *Crossing Over,* he'll make me redo it because there was a wrinkle in my shirt, or a few hairs on my head were out of alignment. At least once a week, he starts a sentence off with "Hey, wouldn't it be *great* if . . . " to which I usually shake my head no, but end up doing it anyway.

Now the tables were turned, and it felt pretty good. I only felt bad about it once during the climb . . . the time Paul was crying for his mommy. Um, okay, I made that last part up. But he did look like he was going to cry for his mom when he was taking his tiny, measured, delicate steps up, moving ever so slowly.

Natasha, a very strong Slavic girl, was behind Paul the whole way and promised to catch him if he fell. We paused at the bridge's highest point, and the views of the harbor were magnificent. Amanda told us stories about the builders who had died while constructing the bridge, and we all stood there high over Sydney, enjoying a panoramic, spiritual moment. For once, I was glad that we'd caught something like that on film. As we began to descend, I looked over at Jill in the group behind us and noticed she was in that same senior-citizen posture Paul had adopted.

"Having fun?" I yelled over to her. And her response was a pleading, "Get me off this thing!" All right, enough was enough. I pulled Amanda aside and asked if we could take a different downward route . . . say, in the elevator? She sweetly agreed to rescue us all, and I told Jill that she owed me big time. The next time she wanted me to walk the press line and I didn't want to do it, all I had to do was give her the magic word: *brrrrrridge!* As we descended (yes, in the elevator!), I thought of the bridge as a metaphor for all our souls' journeys. Regardless of where we are—in a physical body or not—we strive to put one step in front of the other, however tentative, as we travel on our spiritual path.

DO YOU VALIDATE?

I WOKE UP IN MELBOURNE, the last city on the tour, to hear myself being discussed on one of the early-morning talk shows. I was just sort of lazing about in bed flipping the channels when I heard a reporter and the guest astrologer, Athena Starwoman, gabbing about what they thought of me. *Amazing,* I thought. My level of public recognition down under was still difficult for me to grasp. Back home, an ocean away, the talk was all about the impending war. The night before I'd seen Saddam Hussein's son on CNN threatening the U.S. that if we attacked Iraq, the tears we cried over 9/11 would seem "like a picnic" compared to what *will* happen. His words shook me up.

Now I switched channels to CNN again and felt a wave of patriotism for America as I watched our troops hugging their wives, husbands, and kids good-bye and getting on ships going God knows where. It totally put me over the edge when I saw one news clip of a soldier telling a reporter, "You know, my baby son is going to be crawling when I see him next." I thought of Sandra and Justin back home and missed them terribly. I wondered if they were asleep and if it was it too late to call and send good-night kisses over the phone.

I was still feeling pretty emotional as we drove to the convention center that night. When we arrived, our driver couldn't find the proper entrance and turned into the wrong road in front of a locked gate. While we were waiting for him to figure out which way to go, a bunch of religious protesters approached the car holding up signs. Once they realized I was in the car, they began banging on my window for me to roll it down. I've had a few experiences with holy rollers who show up at these events claiming I'm a fraud and it's all entertainment. As I've said, I totally respect the fact that some people don't believe in what I do—it's their choice. But the last thing I felt like hearing that night was someone yelling in my face that I was doing "the devil's work."

Those words in particular make me want to tug off my spiritual gloves and knock the person on their ass. I don't need anyone questioning my faith. And anyway, to me, this work isn't religious, it's spiritual . . . it's painting an energy portrait. Whatever canvas or framework an individual uses to paint that portrait is their choice and based on their own belief system. One person might have a Catholic framework, and another might have a Muslim framework, and somebody might have a Jewish framework, and somebody might have no framework at all because they're atheistic. The atheists, interestingly enough, are usually the loudest energies who come through once they get to the Other Side because they have so much to say after they realize, *Yikes—I was wrong, there is an after-life after all!*

So, needless to say, I didn't roll down my window. I just smiled and waved as we drove away to the proper gate, leaving the protesters muttering to themselves in the parking lot. For the duration of our trip in Australia, these were the only demonstrators I attracted. And before introducing me that night, Leon told the audience he was nicknaming our time down under as "The Silence of the Skeptics Tour" because we'd barely heard a peep from the diehard cynics.

One of the last readings in Australia turned out to be one of the funniest and most dramatic moments on tour. It was for two sisters, Jeannie-Marie and Victoria; and Jeannie's mother-in-law, Carmel. The sisters had come to the seminar together thanks to Victoria's 18-year-old daughter, Kerrina, who had given up her cherished ticket so that the two women could have a night out together. They didn't know that Carmel was in the audience until they saw her face on the giant video screen as I was giving a reading to someone sitting near her. And then, I felt a pull in two opposite directions. . . .

John: I have two families who are split. I have somebody on one side of the room who's connected to somebody
on the other side of the room. So if you know you have family here and you're not sitting next to each other, say, "I'm
over here!"

[A young woman stands up and waves wildly, dancing
around.]

Jeannie: Hi, Mom! I love you!

John: Can somebody claim this child? [Much laughter.
A woman stands up directly on the other side of the room.]

Carmel: That's my daughter-in-law!

What followed was a back-and-forth family reading worthy of
a tennis match at the Australian Open. Carmel's husband, who had
passed from cancer, came through and brought with him the family cat, a child connected to Victoria, and also shed light on a
naughty family romance. I was even able to use my TV pop-culture
reference to unearth more family mysteries.

John: Okay, do you guys know *I Dream of Jeannie?*

Jeannie: That's me! That's my name! [dancing around]

John: But there's more to it than that. In *I Dream of Jeannie,* the astronaut lands his spaceship on a deserted beach,
and *poof,* there's the bottle. There's got to be a story in your
family where your husband landed someplace he thought
might have been deserted, or there had to be some type of
unique landing and then he found out . . . there's a funny
story at the end of that somewhere . . . . where he might
have thought he landed in enemy territory and he landed
on his own Air Force base. Do you know what he means
when he's talking about the unique landing or the funny
story like that?

Carmel: Yes!

John: Can you explain that?

Carmel: No . . . it's private! [more laughter]

The audience had a good time and a lot of laughs with this family reading, but never knew of the dramatic scene that followed later that night. After the seminar, Natasha and Duncan walked Jeannie-Marie and Victoria back to their hotel where Kerrina was waiting. Kerrina was originally going to accompany her mother to the seminar because she was anxious to connect with a childhood friend, Ryan, who had died nine years earlier from leukemia. The women weren't sure how she was going to react when they told her the good news: that they had a reading . . . and the not-as-good news: that Ryan didn't show up.

When the gang reached the hotel, Kerrina, who had been curled up in front of the TV, answered the door in her pajamas.

"You had a reading?" she asked, hopeful, after one glance at their smiling faces. "Who? *Who was it?*" she demanded, excited.

When the women told her that Ryan didn't come through, Kerrina burst into tears.

"But why, Mom? *Where is he? Why didn't he come through?*"

The three women stood in the hallway of the hotel hugging and crying. Natasha and Duncan—pulled into the group hug—tried to console young Kerrina.

Kerrina's disappointment is something I face every time I do a reading. I try to prepare people for the possibility that you won't always hear from those you want to hear from—we don't have control over who comes through. Sometimes it's difficult to find the words to ease the pain.

"He'll be in heaven, darling," Victoria told her daughter, stroking her hair as she sobbed. "There wasn't a message for you this time. It's like John says, not everybody gets a reading, but everybody's in heaven."

What happened next, says Natasha, was a moment as heartfelt as they come—and it carries with it a message with a capital "M" for all of you reading this.

"Kerrina dried her tears with her sleeve, looked up, and smiled," recalled Natasha, "and she realized she'd helped get the reading for her mom, her aunt, and for Carmel, and she was so happy. Here was this teenage kid who suddenly realized how, in this universe, we are all wonderfully connected."

Through her broken heart, Kerrina saw the bigger picture. And in doing so, she was able to be happy for her aunt, who had a reading instead of her because of her selfless act.

"The three of them were meant to be there together," Kerrina said, still sniffling, "and it just wasn't my turn. Not yet."

BY THE END OF THE TRIP, I was tapped out energy-wise, but also exhilarated. I was pleased to find that no matter where we are in this world, the human experience of love and loss is universal. Despite my sporadic fumblings with the down-under dialect, I realized that Australia and America weren't all that different. The spirit world crossed barriers in culture and geography. So far from home, people here were just as anxious to connect with their loved ones, be assured they were okay, and know they weren't so far away after all.

CHAPTER FOUR

Houston

I'VE ONLY BEEN TO HOUSTON, TEXAS, a handful of times in my life, but each time, I've been wowed by the readings I've experienced there—two seminars in particular were especially memorable for me.

The first, in February 2002, was unforgettable because of the unusual way one energy from the Other Side grabbed my attention. I was preparing for the seminar in my usual manner—doing the rosary and meditating—when Ace, one of my security guys that day, knocked on my hotel-room door to check if I was ready. I popped my rosary beads into my pocket, grabbed my sunglasses, and we hopped into the elevator together . . . and that's when it started. I was suddenly distracted—not by the living people coming in and out of the elevator—but instead, by a young girl from the Other Side.

If an energy tries to get through to me when I'm "off duty," so to speak—that is, when I'm not specifically doing a reading or paying focused attention to the Other Side—I'll feel a buzzing at the base of my neck. This can happen before a seminar has begun or even when I'm on vacation, when I'm at the gym . . . it even happened on my honeymoon in the middle of the night (Sandra was a good sport about it). It's like I've turned off or tuned out from my phone line to the Other Side, but I'm on eternal "vibrate" just in case of an emergency.

That buzzing means *pay attention to me!* It started in the elevator, and it followed me through the lobby, out the front door, and into the car. As soon as I buckled my seatbelt, this young girl let the information fly. I saw a picture of a room that looked like a lecture hall. Was it tonight's venue? I had no idea, since I'd never been to this auditorium before. I saw a picture of a large American flag in the back, left-hand section of this room. The young girl told me that she belonged to someone who would soon be sitting in that flag section, and then she continued sending me messages—including one about an organ-donation issue. During the entire drive to the seminar location, this girl wouldn't stop. I was getting pictures and feelings . . . and that buzzing at my neck. So much was coming through so fast, I was afraid I wouldn't remember all the information for the seminar an hour later. So I started to repeat it out loud to Ace as he drove.

Ever since my popularity has escalated, I've had to travel with a security crew whose job it is to check the entrances and exits of venues where I'm appearing and make sure our routes are planned and I stay safe. Ace—a big, muscular, retired court officer—was not only acting as driver and bodyguard this day, he was also trying to help me remember the information bombarding me. I kept getting flashes of this room with the American flag, so I asked Ace if he'd noticed the Stars and Stripes on the back wall as he did the security walk-through of the venue earlier that day. He couldn't remember. I had a hard time believing that he'd forget seeing this humongous flag I was envisioning in my mind if it was there, but of course, Ace's focus is on security—not on the room's decor.

I kept repeating the information over and over to him so that between us, we'd remember it. When energies come through early like this before a seminar, it kind of feels like they're "jumping the line" or "cutting in"—as if they're afraid they won't be able to get through once I'm in front of a big group of people and their respective dead relatives, battling it out for stage time. My guides, who act as my Other Side "security," don't usually allow energies to come through at random times. They put up the Do Not Disturb sign to make sure I can go through my daily routine like everybody else and not be interrupted every morning when I shave or every night at the dinner table. So when energies *do* get through, it means that they've convinced The Boys it's something important enough to warrant special treatment. As far as I'm concerned, whoever gets through to me is *meant* to get through, so whenever this happens, I listen.

As we pulled up to the convention center, Ace noticed a row of flags on the building next door and pointed them out. But I was sure that the flag I was seeing in my mind was *inside* the room, not outside. The girl showed me the image again and then continued throwing information at me. I had to start this reading pronto; this girl wouldn't let me rest. We rushed inside, and when I got backstage, Carol, my assistant, noticed that I was restless.

"What's wrong?" she asked.

"Carol, I have to start the seminar *right away*," I told her. "I have a girl coming through, and she's insisting I start with her—*now*." I told her about the American flag message and asked if she'd seen one in the room. She shook her head no.

"Well . . . anyway, we *have* to start," I said. I was anxious to get this message out of the way and was worried that if I didn't, this energy might mess up the entire seminar. I usually like to lecture for at least an hour before I start doing readings, to familiarize the audience with how I work. If they aren't accustomed to the process and an energy from the Other Side is trying to relay a message and the relatives here don't know how to "receive" it, the whole thing gets very frustrating, and it feels like trying to talk on the phone with a child (in this case, the Other Side) tugging at my sleeve.

But we couldn't start the seminar yet, Carol informed me, because people were still arriving and finding their seats. I put the microphone in her hand and begged her to just introduce me, and do it fast . . . the floodgates were opening, the information was flowing, and I was about to burst.

Carol peeked her head through the black-velvet curtains to check again on the audience. Doing intros was not her usual duty.

She hated speaking in front of large groups of people, and usually we have a local radio personality introduce me. But today it was *her* job, so she was already nervous to begin with. Then, I'd doubled her panic because of the urgency I was feeling at the moment. And now, I was pushing her to start ahead of schedule. Carol walked out onstage, anxious and flustered, and cleared her throat.

Backstage, I did some last-minute meditating. I closed my eyes and silently told this female energy coming through that it was "showtime" for her and her family. I asked her to come through with information to help her family recognize her, and let them know how important it was to her to come through *first*.

"Ladies and gentlemen," I heard Carol say, voice quavering, "Um . . . John is ready to begin immediately . . . uh . . . if you all would please take your seats . . . and please . . . turn off all your cell phones and . . . um . . . vibrators. . . . "

My eyes popped open, and I looked at Ace. "Did Carol just say to turn off your *vibrators?!*" He didn't have to answer. A second later, the audience erupted into thunderous applause at Carol's blunder. Of course she'd intended to say, "Please turn off your cell phones and *put your pagers on vibrate.* . . ." The audience was in hysterics, and I was laughing so hard from backstage that tears were dripping down my face. When Carol returned to where I was waiting, she was a shade of red so bright I laughed even harder. It was a major icebreaker that day, and Carol's flubbed line became a classic story to tell at subsequent seminars.

But now, it was time to get serious and deliver this girl's message. I walked out onto the stage in front of the 2,500 people there and immediately scanned the back, left-hand side of the room, expecting to see the American flag. *No flag.* I paused, a bit surprised. Maybe I'd misinterpreted the message? I began telling the audience what had taken place on the car ride over, hoping that someone would connect with the information I'd been given.

As a medium, I knew I had to surrender my ego and keep going with the information as I saw it, even though I risked being "wrong." My job is to honor those on the Other Side and the information I'm given as it comes to me. I rattled off the details again, looking over at Ace to make sure I was getting it right, and I repeated everything twice as I paced up and down the stage. I looked out to the back section of the room where the flag *wasn't,* and searched the sea of faces in the crowd to see if anyone showed a hint of recognition.

The room was quiet, and everyone was still. Those minutes standing onstage felt like a lifetime, and all I could think was that I'd made a poor decision. As a teacher, which is ultimately how I see my work, maybe I shouldn't have deviated from my normal curriculum. Because I hadn't given my usual explanation of the process, this girl's family might not understand what I was saying, and this message wouldn't make it through. I was kicking myself for making a bad call when very, very slowly, a woman stood up in that section in the back. Everyone turned and gasped. This woman was cloaked in red, white, and blue. She was wearing a big leather bomber jacket in the same shape, design, and colors of the American flag. She then proceeded to validate each and every detail that had come through to me earlier, courtesy of her dear daughter who had crossed over.

HOUSTON, WE HAVE A PROBLEM

ALMOST ONE YEAR TO THE DAY, I was back in Houston. It was a chilly February morning in 2003, and I was fighting a cold but losing the battle. One funny thing about being a medium is that when I do readings while I'm sick, the Other Side suspends my symptoms and carries me through. But when I'm finished the reading, I feel sicker than ever. It's like I use up any reserve fuel I have and am left depleted. I began the seminar by telling the audience the story of the woman wearing the American flag jacket the year before, and many who were present—who were also in attendance the year before—remembered the moment.

This time, I started the seminar in my usual way—giving a talk about how the process works and taking questions from the audience. Some people asked the standard questions about my personal experiences, while others took the microphone to thank me for doing what I do. One woman in particular almost reduced me to tears when she shared that she'd recently lost a baby, and watching *Crossing Over* had become a form of therapy for her in dealing with her overwhelming grief.

When people tell me things like that, I feel an immediate and emotional reaction deep down inside my gut, inside my inner being . . . like I just won the spiritual lottery. But instead of money as the reward, it's joy. When someone appreciates my work, it's truly like they're handing me a gift. It's not easy for me to leave my family behind and travel from city to city as much as I do—so often that I sometimes forget what city I'm in. So when someone takes the time to communicate with, appreciate, and validate *me* . . . well, I just melt into a mushy puddle. So, thank you to all the people out there who have done that for me. It makes all the sweat and the B.S. that sometimes comes with this work worth it.

As soon as the lecture and Q&A period were over, I was pulled to the middle section of the room. I remember standing on the stage of the theater, extending my arm out in front of me and pointing— drawing a straight line from me to the center of the audience. As I did so, I had a powerful image in my mind's eye . . . it was the Columbia space shuttle. I just knew . . . I *knew* . . . this message coming through had something to do with the explosion that had occurred just three weeks earlier, and someone right in front of me was connected to it.

My own connection to this disaster began before it even happened. I'd watched the shuttle take off on television on January 16 from home with Sandra, and I remember getting a really bad feeling as it shot into the sky. It was just a general "not good" feeling— nothing specific. That's how I often feel these kinds of premonitions—my guides don't show me details. So when people ask why I don't do anything to prevent some tragedy, that's my answer: I don't know myself what's going to happen.

Five days later in Los Angeles, en route to Australia, I did a magazine interview, and the reporter asked me if I get premonitions, and could I give her my most recent one. I said sure, but it wasn't a very positive one. I told her that I'd watched the Columbia launch and felt concern for the astronauts. The reporter immediately jumped on it and asked, "Is it going to crash? Or explode?" and I freaked out a bit, realizing maybe I'd said too much. I tried to backpedal a bit to calm us both down, saying, "No, no . . . I just don't have a good feeling."

That was the last I thought about the shuttle until the final night in Australia, on January 29, 2003, when we had a huge dinner in Melbourne with all the people who had helped organize the tour, as well as the Hay House Australia team—my new Aussie family. Natasha and I were digging into our steaks and making idle chitchat about the local wine when I froze mid-sentence, fork in air.

"John . . . what's wrong?" Natasha asked. She recognized that *look* on my face.

"I feel like something is exploding," I told her, putting my fork down—"and there's some kind of . . . Israeli connection to it."

What? When? *Where?* She asked about a dozen reporter-like questions, whipping out her pen and notebook, but I couldn't answer any of them because I didn't know the answers myself. I told her not to worry about it for now, and I pushed the feeling out of my mind. I kind of thought, okay . . . Israel . . . they have explosions there all the time . . . this isn't so psychic of me. We both went to sleep that night a little uneasy.

The next day we boarded the plane for the long flight back home. As we waited for our connecting flight in Los Angeles, there it was on CNN. The shuttle had exploded that morning, killing its entire seven-member crew—including the first Israeli in history to ever make that expedition. Sitting in the airport that morning, I felt the deep sadness I always experience when a bad premonition comes true, and I said a silent prayer for the crew members and their families.

"I feel really awkward saying this," I told the audience in Houston, "but is there someone here connected with someone who perished in the recent shuttle disaster?"

There was an immediate hush over the room. I felt uncomfortable asking this question because the time frame was so close to the disaster, and I was sure that anyone connected would still be emotionally raw. I always tell people that mediumship is not a cure for grief, and can only be helpful at the right time during a person's journey *through* this grief—which is rarely right after their loved one has passed.

I discourage people from seeing a medium right after a loss. I used to think this was because a person/energy who recently left their body for the Other Side wouldn't be "ready" to come through yet—maybe they first need time to rest up and adjust to their new world. But now, I think the un-readiness has more to do with us here. Right after a person crosses, the loved ones left behind are usually devastated, and they feel a gaping hole in their hearts. It's important to "honor" this pain. And when I say "honor," I don't mean that you should be all happy about it or throw a party. I mean you must let the grief evolve through you naturally—that is, you should feel the pain, cry into a pillow, yell and scream and over-sleep, and most important, work with a counselor, therapist, support group, priest, rabbi, minister—anyone who can help you get through this and get to the core of the hurt.

Once you get to the core of the pain, you can start finding your way back out again. And for each person, this journey through pain—then beyond it—is a unique, important, and healing experience. If someone seeks out a reading too early, it may interfere with their natural stages of grief—which can take months or years, depending on the person.

In my novel, *What If God Were the Sun?*, I explored this journey through the life of a fictional family. I stress the word *fictional*, because many people, even some of my family members, thought it was autobiographical. Yes, there were hints of my family in there, but it was more an amalgamation of the many families I've sat down with and read over the years.

In the novel, the family learns about "honoring their grief" and how grief is really the other side of love. Think about it: Your love for a person is like a flow of energy, and it's directed from you to them. But when the person dies—or when their *body* dies—many of us don't know where to put the love/energy anymore, and it gets backed up. This causes a blockage of energy within us, and this blockage locks our grief. Understanding their death, honoring it, accepting it, and walking that long road through grief helps us move through that blockage and then understand that our loved ones are still a *part* of our lives—not *apart* from our lives.

When we move through the blockage, we get back to the love. For those of you who have experienced severe loss, you're well aware that you never get over that loss entirely. You get *through* it, and it changes you. Those who haven't lost a loved one can't understand this feeling, and often say to those who are grieving: "Aren't you over it yet? He's in a better place now. It's better this way . . . she's out of pain." If you don't know what to say to a friend or loved one in pain, just say: "I'm here for you." Those four words are helpful.

Back to the reading in Houston. I was hesitant to bring up the shuttle disaster for fear that the loss was too recent, but my main rule in this work is: *If they show it, so do I.* A big part of the process is not editing what I get.

"Someone right in that section," I said, pointing out front, "is connected with one of the astronauts who crossed on the space shuttle Columbia three weeks ago." A woman directly in front of me, in the very back of the room, stood up.

"My husband is Rick Husband's cousin," she said.

I didn't know whom she was talking about, since I didn't know the names of the astronauts. The woman explained that Rick Husband was the commander of the Columbia, and a cousin by marriage. Once she validated this, the information started to flow. Rick said that there would be additional information about the disaster that the families of the astronauts would be receiving—perhaps a video, which may or may not become public knowledge. There were also "audible" messages of the shuttle crew on tape that the public didn't know about yet, but would soon. I was shown that the passing of the astronauts was fast and somewhat of a surprise, and they were unconscious before anything happened to their physical bodies.

"It's as if they were asleep," I told the audience, as I dropped my head to the side in a sleeping position to show what I was feeling and seeing. Everyone applauded at that, in relief for the astronauts and their families.

"Rick comes from a religious family . . . " was the next bit of information I got. The entire room nodded in unison. Everyone seemed to know this about their hometown son except me.

"There's an 'LN' name . . . like Lynne . . . connected to Rick. Is this you?"

She shook her head no. And then I felt a split pull—as if I were a sheet of paper torn in half and separated in two opposite directions.

"Is there someone else here in the room who also knows Rick? Or is there someone else here connected to *another* member of the shuttle crew?"

A petite woman about ten rows in front of me raised her hand. "Yes," she said, "I knew the Israeli astronaut on that flight, Ilan [pronounced *Ee-LAN*]."

Okay, so that explained the "Lynne" name. For me, when I hear names that start with a vowel, I will not hear that first vowel. I'll hear the consonant sounds following the vowel as strong and predominant. So in this case, "Ilan" became more of a "Lan" or "Lin" sound in my head, because I didn't hear the "E" sound. Information started coming through from this second astronaut.

"He wants me to acknowledge his kids . . . and something about the music. Was someone singing either to him from here, or was he singing to here from there?"

"He and his wife had a song about being far away," the woman answered in an emotional whisper, "and she sang it to him while he was there." At this point, I was getting emotional, too.

"And his daughter, his little girl," the woman continued, "watched her father take off in the shuttle. And at that moment, she said out loud, 'I just lost my daddy.'"

All right, now I was doing everything possible to keep myself from losing it right there onstage. Normally when I do readings, I can stay detached from the feeling part of it—that's how I'm able to relay such poignant details time after time without becoming a sobbing wreck. But this last image of the astronaut's little girl waving good-bye to her daddy just got me. Ever since my Justin had been born, readings that deal with parent-child relationships have an even deeper and more heartbreaking effect on me than before.

After the event, Carol told me that it was highly publicized and reported in the newspapers that the astronaut's daughter had said those words as the shuttle blasted off. So did the little girl sense what was going to happen? Well, I do believe our soul decides when it's completed its lessons here in the physical world. And when that time comes, we allow ourselves to exit. Some events, which we call "accidents," may not be accidents at all in terms of the Other Side.

I'd describe it more like this: Let's say you're on a business trip and you've finished your meetings early, but your flight home isn't until the next day. You might try to hop on an earlier flight to get home sooner. If you do, it was your decision to alter your path. I believe that the soul makes that same decision to change its journey, to go *home* home—to its spiritual home. Some people, often children, can be aware when it's time for a soul to leave this world. What that little girl experienced is nothing short of a gift, and to me, it's clear she was given a validation that it was her dad's *time*.

Think about the people you love who have crossed over. If it wasn't a long illness that brought them to the Other Side, and it was more of a sudden event, examine what they were doing or saying during the months leading up to the moment they physically left. You might discover clues that their soul was getting ready to "go home." Maybe the person recently gave away a treasured piece of jewelry or reconciled with an estranged friend. Maybe they got all their paperwork in order and wrote a will. The soul knows it's getting ready to leave, and that unconscious thought flows into our everyday lives. After reading dozens of September 11 families in the last year and a half, I can tell you that I've seen examples of this over and over. Both the energies coming through, and their loved ones here, often talk about signs—whether spoken or acted out—that signaled they were going to leave.

BY THE END OF THOSE TWO READINGS in Houston, the astronauts had also brought through the parents of the two women. I hope that they found comfort in that, and in knowing that the astronauts saw them as an opportunity to pass on messages to their loved ones here and let them know they're okay.

Two weeks after the seminar, on March 1, news reports validated the information that came through in the reading. The New York *Daily News* revealed that a video had been found in Texas showing the crew's last moments—laughing, talking, and not knowing anything was wrong. It was "a remarkable fragment of video that survived the terrible fires that consumed the space shuttle Columbia," the report said. "There is not even a hint of concern, anxiety—nothing . . . trauma specialists said the cheerful images would bring comfort to the families, who were shown the video and agreed it should be made public."

SPIRITUAL MAIL CARRIER

A MONTH AFTER MY STAY IN HOUSTON, I was contacted by Nancy Marlowe Sheppard, Rick Husband's relative whom I'd read at the seminar. Sheppard, a retired school teacher, was eager to tell me what had happened to her before she even got to the reading that day. Ever since the shuttle explosion, she'd been having strong feelings that she needed to attend a taping of *Crossing Over*—that if she did, something important might happen. When she learned about the seminar that was to happen nearby, she called the venue to get a ticket but was told it had been sold out for months.

Nancy recalled, "I said to the woman on the phone, 'Look, I *really* need to go. Can't you try again?'"

Often, I believe, the Other Side really does have a hand in getting people where they need to be. In many cases, people who have tried to get tickets for the *Crossing Over* gallery, or for a seminar or private reading, often get them as a fluke or seemingly by "coincidence"—and they end up having a dramatic reading.

But, once again, I don't believe anything is ever a coincidence—the ticket agent suddenly "found" two tickets for Nancy to the sold-out seminar. As she was preparing to leave her house for the event, she had hopes that her deceased parents might come through that day. But before she left home, Nancy had what can only be described as a premonition: Rick's energy came through to her. "I felt Rick's presence," she said, "and I knew he was going to come through at the reading." Her premonition included information that "he and the rest of the crew did not suffer and were grateful for the love America had shown to them."

The message surprised Nancy, but it wasn't a complete shock. "I've always been intuitive," she said, "ever since I was a child. But I always pushed away the hunches, the feelings, the visions, the knowing." It's not uncommon for many people to feel in touch with the spiritual world—whether they get a thought, hear a voice, or smell a whiff of perfume that Mom used to wear—most people at one time or another have had psychic experiences. We all have this ability within us to different degrees, but rather than pay attention to it, many ignore it. Nancy had tried to ignore her "hunches" her entire life, but on the day of the reading, she couldn't do it anymore.

"I was sitting in the second-to-last row, in the last seat. I know you couldn't even see me from up on the stage," recalled Nancy. "When you asked if there was anyone related to the Columbia crew and I stood up, I was the only one standing in the room, and my heart was beating so fast. I told you I was connected to Rick, and then you said, 'Rick Husband is *here*.' One of the messages you got was that Rick was a religious man—and it's true. He went to church, he spoke in Sunday school, and did all sorts of things like that. And then my parents came through in the reading. . . . "

Nancy was overjoyed that her mom and dad came through and made a "cameo appearance," giving accurate family birthdays, anniversaries, and illnesses so that she knew it was them. But what affected her most was something I said to the group at the end of the evening.

Nancy remembered, "You paused, and then you said, 'Did someone here know *before* the seminar that this was going to happen?' That's the part that was so awesome for me. I was still standing, and I said, 'I knew!'"

A month after the seminar, Nancy sent a letter to Rick's mother and wife to tell them about her experience, and as this book goes to print, Nancy hadn't heard back from them yet but is hoping that the words gave them peace. That day in Houston was Nancy's introduction to being a "spiritual mail carrier." It began with her premonition earlier in the day and continued with her delivering a message for the Other Side when she mailed that letter to Rick's family.

Being a spiritual mail carrier is a job many of us undertake although we may not be aware of it. The young girl watching her father leave on the shuttle was passing along a message, too. You don't need to be a medium to work with the Other Side; you just need to be open to the vibrations and be willing to listen.

"I really think I was supposed to be there," Nancy continued. "I think that's why I got the ticket at the last minute. I think Rick Husband knew I'd be there and chose me to get his message out."

CHAPTER FIVE

Telephone Tag

SOME READINGS FLOW EASILY, with information coming through from the Other Side clearly, and the sitter recognizing the details immediately. Other sessions can be more of a challenge, and there are a number of reasons why. First, I might be interpreting the information incorrectly, like in the instance I spoke of earlier when I got the gun-taxicab image and thought a young man had been murdered in a taxi, when he was actually shot in the front part—the "cab"—of a truck. That's an example of how I'm shown images by the Other Side that could take on a number of meanings, and my immediate interpretation is one meaning when it's actually another.

Second, a sitter might not be approaching a session with an open mind. Some people are determined to hear from certain people and assume that they'll say certain things, closing their brain off to other possibilities. Sure, you might want to hear from Uncle Harry and hope he'll tell you where the family treasure is stashed. But instead, the guy who had a crush on you in college comes through and jokes about how you cheated on that French exam. But you don't recognize this guy because you only want to hear from Uncle Harry. When this happens, it doesn't matter how hard the energies or I work to open your eyes—nothing will make you see. And then you go home disappointed, assuming that the process just "didn't work" for you.

Sometimes a reading is off because what's coming through isn't intended for you. Usually after a bit of confusion and a few minutes—if we're lucky—we discover that the information is actually for a friend, co-worker, or relative. If possible, we get that person on the phone, and when we do, the validations again flow like the Mississippi.

Other times, a reading gets jammed up and I can't pinpoint the problem. The information is coming through to me clearly, but the sitter doesn't understand it for herself or for anyone else she knows. This is what happened during a recent phone reading I did with a very nice woman named Deanna, a medical reporter in Chicago, who was hoping to connect with her young son who had passed away a few years earlier.

During the reading, the information struck me with the force and clarity of a hardball hitting me in the gut. I was sure of it. But for the most part, that ball dropped to the ground with a *thud*. Deanna couldn't connect with what I was telling her. In most readings, if a detail can't be validated, it's no big deal. I try to reinterpret the message or we call up a family member—and if those two things don't work, I insist that the sitter write it down to check later, and then we move onward.

Often, the sitter calls me weeks or months later to tell me— *Aha!*—they figured it out A string of non-validations during a reading do become a problem, however, when the energy is insistent and will not let it go. Because then I get persistent myself, which frustrates the sitter, and all three parties get caught up in a three-way wrestling match of spiritual proportions. For example:

> **John:** Somebody's claiming that their actions brought about their passing, which for me would be like somebody taking responsibility for how they crossed. This doesn't encompass an actual suicide, but is like a weird passing where somebody is slightly responsible for it.

Deanna: No . . .

John: Uh, *yes.* You just might not be aware of it, or it might hit you later, but I assure you this is definitely connected to you.

[Then later in the reading, it comes up again.]

John: Okay . . . there's somebody who's claiming that their actions brought about their passing.

Deanna: No . . .

John: Well, I'm gonna disagree again.

[The issue comes up a third time later.]

John: Okay, are you positive there's nobody in that family who crossed themselves over, or something that they did caused how they passed?

Deanna: I'm positive.

John: Well, again I'm going to disagree.

John: Were your son and his dad at odds?

Deanna: No.

John: He's making me feel an issue about dealing with Dad and being at odds. Also, I'm supposed to be talking about Mark, or Marky.

Deanna: No . . .

John: Oh, *yes.*

Deanna: I can't think of anyone.

John: Would he have a male figure to his side, like a good friend who got married or celebrated something after he left?

Deanna: No.

John: Are you positive?

Deanna: Positive.

John: Really? He's harping on this. Was he an insistent energy? I mean, was he somebody who would not drop things?

Deanna: No.

John: Okay, they're telling me to go straight north. So, to me, I want to go to upstate New York . . . I want to go to Canada . . .

Deanna: No.

John: There must be some ties. They're trying to get me to get you someplace north to understand what's coming through.

Deanna: No, I don't understand that.

John: I know you don't. That's why I keep saying the same thing over again, because they're trying really hard to get me to get you where they want, and that's up north. And they're also claiming somebody just passed. Did you just lose a cousin or an aunt?

Deanna: No.

John: Are you sure?

Deanna: I'm positive.

John: Oh, I think you're wrong. This is the part of my job that I absolutely hate, like talking to a complete stranger and now arguing with her about her family! [laughs] This stuff is not changing . . . I went through like seven pages already on the same stuff. Let me start over.

The reading went on like this for a while, and both of us were sighing and trying to focus. I know it sounds illogical for me to be telling someone she's wrong about her own family, but when the same thing is shown to me repeatedly from the Other Side, I become that bulldog. Thankfully, sprinkled within the confusion in Deanna's reading, her son did come through, and we got some specific, intimate family details that rang true as a bell and ended the session on a very happy note for both of us.

IF YOU'RE THINKING THAT DEANNA'S READING was a challenge because it was over the phone, that's a common misconception. Most people imagine that if I'm going to communicate with someone who's "dead," I'd at least need their living, breathing relative to be sitting in front of me in the flesh. Not so. Ever since I started this work, I've done phone readings for clients who couldn't travel to my office. I also routinely do phone sessions when I'm a guest on radio or television shows where people call into the show to be read over the air.

Whether the session is face-to-face, on the phone, or even over the Internet—which I've also done—it all works the same way . . . with energy. And energy knows no distance.

To understand how it works, you first need to be aware that the energies that come through to me are connected to *you,* the person I'm reading—not to myself. Their home base isn't around me or my office or at the studio where I shoot *Crossing Over.* The energies surround and sort of "travel" with the person they "belong" to . . . whom they're connected to on this earth. (I don't say this to freak you out. Don't worry, they aren't lingering and leering in the bathroom every time you take a shower. They have other things to do.)

So the energies are linked to you, and then they try to get my attention because, first, they know I can hear them; and second, they know I'm talking to you and keying into you and the energies around you. Whether the reading is in person or on the phone, I get the messages in a similar fashion. If it's in person, the energies around you as you sit in front of me vie for my attention and say, "Hey, John . . . over here!" It's the same on the phone. Imagine that I'm chatting with you on the phone and you're at home, and one of your family members yells over your shoulder into the phone, "Yo, John . . . over here!" Same deal. I hear it in the same way. All of our energies connect whether I'm two feet or 200 miles away from you.

Just to show you that the phone line had nothing to do with the hurdles in Deanna's session, here's another reading I did over the phone just one hour before Deanna's. If we were to consider this a phone "experiment," we might say that I was the constant, and the sitters and the Other Side were the variables. I don't know how these variables differed from each other, but as you'll see, the two readings were poles apart.

The first reading, as I found out afterward, was with writer Norris Church Mailer, wife of two-time Pulitzer Prize–winning novelist Norman Mailer. Norris telephoned my office in Huntington, New York, from her home in Provincetown, Massachusetts, and I conferenced-in Natasha from her apartment in Manhattan.

Natasha had organized both Deanna's and Norris's sessions and was listening in on the other end of the three-way phone chats, taking notes and tape-recording the exchanges. (Of course, we'd checked in with Natasha during Deanna's reading to see if any of the unvalidated information was for her—it wasn't.) It was just as important to Natasha, a seasoned news reporter, as it was to me to know that the integrity of the readings remained intact and that I knew nothing about the person or whom they were trying to connect with.

As you'll see, the loved one Norris wanted to hear from the most came through right away, and with tremendous clarity—that is, until the reading took a surprising turn and the Other Side came through with an unexpected gift. You may have noticed during some of the episodes of *Crossing Over* that anyone in my energy area—either physically or on the phone—has the potential to be read. It happened during Norris's reading, and in this case, it was someone else on the phone line. From the get-go, an energy came through—a mother figure with a "MAR" name—who wasn't connected to Norris. For a moment, we were confused.

But in this case, the mix-up was sorted out right away.

Little did I know that Natasha had lost her mother, Maria, ten years earlier . . . and here was Mom showing up while her daughter was busy at work so she could say hello to her little girl.

I'd known Natasha professionally for four years (as a journalist, she'd interviewed me several times), and we'd become friends in the last year, yet she'd never told me that her mother had passed. Why? She hid this bit of information from her psychic buddy, she told me later, because she was secretly hoping to one day have a reading of her own and didn't want to divulge any of her pertinent Other-Side details. During the dozens of seminars she attended since we started writing this book together, she was always hopeful that her mother would come through at some point, but each time, Natasha left the sessions with notebooks full of readings for other people and not herself. When she finally came to terms with the fact that it would only happen when it was meant to—*it happened.*

John: The first thing I'm going to tell you is that I have an older male coming through, and to me, I would see that being the father figure, the uncle, the grandfather . . .

Norris: Okay.

John: And I don't know if this would be a father figure— like Dad for you, but I'm going to tell you I have a ten connection that comes up. Ten to me means October . . . or the tenth of a month . . . it's a birthday, anniversary. They're also telling me to talk about Mary or Marie. There's an "M-a-r" name that they want me to acknowledge that's connected to the family. I don't believe it's his name, but I believe he is either with "Mar" on the Other Side, or he's acknowledging her as being there. He's also making me feel like, I don't know how to put it, but . . . did you just have a cancer scare?

Norris: Yes.

John: Okay, because they're making me feel like you just went through something that would be like a cancer scare. I literally feel like I'm going into this tunnel, and you're saying to yourself there's no life in here. Okay, but this is a tunnel—I'm going to eventually get to the Other Side. And you kept venturing inside this tunnel, and there's still no life. And the darkness that I have all around this, to me feels like we're going through a very scary place. I have to tell you that they don't think you're out of that place yet, by the way.

Norris: Yes.

John: I feel like you're still there and you're still moving. I feel like you're 80 percent—85 percent through the tunnel, and you can now start to see a little light at the end, but what you need to hear from him is that as long as you keep your eyes closed, you can't tell that you're in the dark, so it's a matter of keeping your eyes closed and walking straight ahead, and allowing your faith to guide you . . . with what you're dealing with and what you're moving forward with. You follow what I'm saying?

Norris: Yes.

John: Now, I don't know if your birthday is in June, but I feel like I need to talk about the celebration or the congratulations that happened in the sixth month. So either this person is aware of what's happening in June, or what happened in June.

Norris: Okay.

John: I also have somebody else coming through. The first gentleman, I think, passes from a health-care-related illness. This other person I'm getting passes in an event, something massive. So whether this was a very bad car accident or they had some type of impact of some sort . . . I want to talk about an explosion. There's a Chris that I'm supposed to bring up around this. I don't know if the person I'm talking about is Chris, or they're connected to Chris or Chrissie or Christine, but there's like a Chris connection that comes up with it, and they're telling me to tell you 15. So the 15th has to be linked to this whole thing. To me it feels like this could be a contemporary of you. Or the first gentleman we talked about, it might be a contemporary to him. There is this Chrissie, Chris, Christine, "C" or "K" connection that comes up, but then there's a big boom. Is there a Robert connected to you? A Robert or Robbie or Roberta that might be connected to your side of the family?

Norris: I can't think of any Robert, but that doesn't mean there's not one.

John: Okay, hold on one second. I want to go back . . . no, no I don't. I want to stay here. Hold on. Your mom's passed?

Norris: No.

John: I have someone here who's claiming to be Mom. Wait, wait, wait. Hold on. She's claiming to be connected to Robert. She's connecting herself to what I just said—this whole impact, Chris, the number 15, the "R" name like Robert, and the mom energy is all linking itself together for me.

Norris: None of that is ringing bells for me. The other stuff definitely rang all the bells.

Natasha: Um . . . John? It makes sense to me. . . .

John: What makes sense to you?

Natasha: Mom passed, and a Robert.

John: Robert's connected to you?

Natasha: Yes.

John: Is Robert still here?

Natasha: Yes. My brother.

John: Okay, then, where does the Chris or Christine or Christopher come up?

Natasha: That part doesn't make sense to me.

John: Okay, there's a definite "C" or "K" connection, there's a 15 connection, which to me means date-wise of the 15th of the month, or that someone was 15 years old. There's a definite explosion of some sort, as if somebody passed in an impact. But if there was an impact, then something fiery had to happen at the same time. It's kinda like it's gruesome—but that's where they're going with this. It all seems connected. Natasha, the mom energy—your mom's passed?

Natasha: Yes . . . and, just a moment . . . my mother's last name has "Chris" in it.

John: In the beginning?

Natasha: Yep. Her last name was Christoff.

John: Okay, that would make sense. Your mom had cancer?

Natasha: Yes.

John: Okay, then I need to tell you that there had to be either three or four hospitalizations, or three or four different types of procedures or things that she had to deal with that would be in conjunction with her type of cancer.

Natasha: Correct.

John: And there had to be some type of false hope, I mean massive false hope, like one of the opportunities going into this, they thought, okay, they got it. And then

I feel like it just flips to the opposite end very, very quickly. I'm also gonna tell you that the 23rd is connected.

Natasha: That's her birthday—March 23rd.

John: Ok, um . . . I never knew your mom passed, Natasha!

Natasha: I don't tell you everything!

John: Do you keep a picture of her on your desk, to the left?

Natasha: Uh, no, I'm looking, I don't see one. . . .

John: How about reader #1. [laughs] Do you have anything near you?

Norris: I have a picture of my father. It's sorta to my right.

John: What's kinda funny is that your dad and Natasha's mother are battling for time here!

Natasha: We thought this might happen!

John: This is funny. Had they known each other in life?

Norris and Natasha: No . . .

John: I want to go back to Dad for a second. I don't know if your dad has the "J" or "G" connection—

Norris: J.

John: He wants to talk about the two boys.

Norris: Yes!

John: He's also making me feel like he has his brother with him, by the way

Norris: Oh, good!

John: He also wants to acknowledge your mom and a sister.

Norris: He has a sister who's alive, yes.

John: He's making me feel like he's got somewhat of a—I don't call it sarcastic, but he's got a quiet way of making a point.

Norris: Yes, exactly.

John: I don't know if you're his baby, but he's making me feel like you're the youngest, or you're the baby girl, or you're the only girl.

Norris: Yup, yup.

John: He tells me to remind you about the rotten eggs, the smelly eggs, making bad eggs, or doing something with eggs.

Norris (laughing): Is it eggs Benedict?

John: It's a bad egg thing for you, for him, whatever . . . like you made them for him, or he made them for you. He's saying to go back to 1992. So 1992 has got to be a turning point for your family. I also feel like your dad either had a military background or there has to be some type of military connection.

Norris: Yes, yes.

John: What he's showing me is some really cool military stuff. There's a trunk, and in the trunk there might be his flag, his pictures, his patches, his this, his that, but there's a coin collection. A few coins, a few medals, or medallions. Is this a recent passing?

Norris: Last July.

John: Okay, to me that's a recent passing. Natasha, your mom's gone for a while? Like just over ten years?

Natasha: Exactly ten years.

John: There was an issue, I believe, well, I'm attaching it to your mom, but if it's your dad, let me know. There's an issue about teeth, or an issue about problems with gums, teeth, the bleeding . . . teeth falling out . . .

Norris: My father had teeth problems.

John: Yep, we've got parents dueling this out now, guys! Um, I do feel that your dad either struggled to leave, or there was a difficulty in some capacity with him leaving.

Norris: Yes.

John: This might not have been an easy passing, just so you know. If you were there watching it, you would know what I'm talking about. Okay, this might be weird, but did you ever see the musical *Dreamgirls?* There's that song, "And I am telling you, I'm not going, I'm stayin' . . . "

Norris: Yeah, yeah, yeah.

John: When he left, he left without saying good-bye or without letting two people see him.

Norris: Yes!

John: And he knows that it was very difficult on the two of them, because they didn't get a chance to bring closure. He did that for their best interest.

Norris: We know he did . . .

John: Okay, because he does not feel that they would have been able to handle the passing, number one; and number two, I think it would have been very difficult for him to be able to leave with them being there or having them there.

Norris: Yeah, he sent us away so he could leave.

John: Yeah, it's not uncommon, it's not uncommon at all. A lot of times they just need that private time to be able to leave, to know that it's okay. Your dad is making me feel that his voice is very raspy. He's making me feel that he had a very difficult time communicating. Either he was on a respirator or there was some type of breathing apparatus that would have made it harder to hear him. And he's saying to tell you "Charlie." So I don't know if Charlie is his friend, but he's telling me to acknowledge Charlie. I almost want to go as far as saying that there's a financial connection—it might just be his way of saying that when you go back and you talk to your mom, and you talk to the family and say did Dad know a Charlie, they'll say yes, a guy he worked with.

Norris: He used to work for a man named Charles.

John: These are the little trivial details that to me are so significant. Now he's telling me that his sister is in a different state than either of us. He says she's a tough lady.

Norris: [laughs] Yes, she is!

John: She's a tough lady. He's telling me to tell you to pass this on, because she might be a little like, *You talked to who, who does what? Oh, I don't know if I believe in all that crap.* But she'll listen. Now the reason why she'll listen is I think she lost a son.

Norris: I don't think so . . . but it's possible.

John: Your dad is acknowledging a younger energy connected to the sister. So she might have miscarried a boy; she might have had a child that passed that the family doesn't know about. It needs to be acknowledged that the younger male is there as well. The only other way I can interpret this would be if Natasha's mom lost a son.

Natasha: Not that I know of.

John: Okay, if your mother has a nephew or a grandson who has passed, then that can be of significance because I need to acknowledge if the younger male is there.

Natasha: She has a brother who died as a child.

John: Younger than her?

Natasha: No, he was older.

John: Then that's not it. So I'm gonna leave it with her dad. Are they southwest of me?

Norris: Yes.

John: Okay, because they're making me feel like it's— geography's not my best—but they're taking me straight down and over to my left a little bit.

Norris: Yup, yup, yup—it's Arkansas.

John: Now, is Lynn connected to you? They're making me feel like I have to say it's an "L-N" name like Lynette, Lynnie, Lenore, Leon. It's like an "L-N" name . . .

Norris: I do know someone named Lynn who just passed.

John: Your dad is making me feel that I need to acknowledge the "L-N" name. I feel like I need to let you know that this person's there as well.

Norris: Okay.

John: Okay, now, I don't know—you definitely have had a two-year tumultuous period.

Norris: Right.

John: I mean we're talking like a *major* emotional, mental, spiritual roller coaster.

Norris: Yes.

John: Your dad wants me to tell you that you need to be happier, like you need to be . . . I mean, I don't want to sound all "foo-foo" here, but I really feel like you need to be a little more appreciative of the smaller things. I don't know if you're a control freak, but I feel that you were trying to dominate and control everything, and you won't be able to, you know. If you're so busy juggling everything, you're gonna drop the things that are right in front of you that need your attention.

Now I don't know if your husband's been traveling a lot for business—

Norris: That's where he is now.

John: Okay. But your dad is making me feel like there's immense, immense traveling that's going to be coming up real soon. So if he traveled twice a year last year, guess what? He's traveling like ten times this year.

Norris: Oh, yeah.

John: Now is Michael, Mikey, connected to you?

Norris: My stepson, Michael—I call him Mikey.

John: Okay, 'cause your dad has told me to acknowledge the Michael or the Mikey as part of his family, so it's important that you know that he sees that as being his family. You're having a hard time dealing with your dad's passing from what he's showing me, is that true?

Norris: Yes.

John: He's making me feel that . . . he's stepping forward . . . and when someone steps forward in a session, it's usually their way of letting me know *why* the session's happening. He's making me feel like people did what they had to do leading up to his passing. People said the things they needed to say . . .

Norris: Okay . . .

John: And some of the people who were there weren't as verbal. I don't think you were very verbal with your dad when he was passing. I don't think you said to him, "It's okay to go, we're gonna be okay, I love you." I don't think you did any of that, but you know what? You didn't have to, because it's not how your family dynamic is set up. The fact that you were there, that spoke volumes.

He does want you to highlight his sister. So I don't know if she's the older sister or if she's the—

Norris: Younger.

John: Well, he's making me feel like she's the matriarch.

Norris: Yeah, she's the youngest, but she *is* the matriarch.

John: She feels like she's the matriarch, you know. I see the mother from Dallas, and that's the matriarch.

Norris: Yes, yes, yes, the boss!

John: The buck stops there. And she knows it, by the way.

Norris: [laughing] Yes.

John: Now, does your mother live in the area?

Norris: She's near me.

John: She has something like a respiratory thing going on?

Norris: No, I don't think so . . .

John: But she has—like asthma or something or—

Norris: Yes.

John: Okay, you're going to have to watch something around her. This could be minor, this could be the beginning of a chest cold, it could be something that she's developing. I don't know exactly what this is, but they're showing me . . . like, *caution*—and I'm always saying I'm not a doctor, I can't diagnose, but they're showing me a yellow light flashing, and they're putting it over her chest.

Norris: Okay.

John: Your dad is telling me to tell you that where you are sitting . . . are you like holding the phone to your right ear?

Norris: Left ear.

John: All right, okay . . . but are you playing with your ear? Or with the hair on the right side . . . ?

Norris: [laughing] Yes!

John: Because he wants to make sure you know he's with you and he's not with me. So he's telling me to tell you he knows what it is you're doing.

Norris: [lots of laughing] Oh my God, I'm twisting my hair!

John: And he's saying to let you know that he's there, and he's still around. He's pulling his energy back.

Natasha, your mom's making me feel like she had to wait to do this. And she doesn't make me feel like anything was impeding her from being able to do this before. But you needed to be at a certain place in your spiritual development . . . whatever this means for you. She does say that her mother is there, so her mom's dead, too?

Natasha: Yep.

John: And she's telling me that you have . . . not disowned your roots, that's not my feeling . . . but I feel you have not taken something that you were supposed to take. Something is yours, but you have not taken it to your house. So if Grandma has a broach that was passed down to your mom, which is now supposed to be passed down to you—you haven't taken it. I don't care if it's a cup, a dish, a fork, a knife, I have no idea what it is, but it's tangible, and you don't have it. I don't know. . . .

You're mom's saying that she pre-deceased one of her own parents?

Natasha: A mother-in-law.

John: She's claiming that she met one of her parents. Like she passed, and then one of her parents passed, because she helped cross that parent over. So if you told me that your dad's mom passed after your mom, that would make sense.

Natasha: Yes, that's exactly right.

John: Okay, I'm also going to tell you that not your mom, but someone above her, one of your grandparents or one of your great-aunts, either suffered from Alzheimer's or had some type of dementia while they were here, because I'm seeing, "I've got my faculties back, I've got everything back." That's connected to the Betty, or the "B" name like Betty or Betsy or something "B"-related. I think that's on your dad's side.

Natasha: My dad's father was going through that. My dad is a "B" name—Basil.

John: And there are three or four important dates in December for your family, Natasha. Like around Christmas. So you could have three birthdays, three anniversaries, three things that take place in the month of December for the family.

Natasha: Yes! We have three birthdays.

John: What is today? Today is February what?

Natasha: 18th? 19th?

John: Now, I know it's not *your* birthday, Natasha.

Natasha: Right . . . that's very good . . . there is a birth-day—

John: Yes, there is a birthday like *now*—

Natasha: There's a birthday today! I made a birthday call . . .

John: Okay, because they're telling me to acknowl-edge the white rose, because they showed that to me before you called me. I know it's not yours, but I want you to know that your mom is seeing the birthday around now.

Natasha: That's amazing! It's her sister's birthday.

John: She's telling me to tell you . . . and I want you to hear this very clearly—this is not the first and this will not be the last time you hear from her. I want to let you know that she's made connections to you previously, which either means you didn't acknowledge it or you just ration-alized it away. . . .

Natasha: Right.

John: The group reading you did . . . she's not making me feel that she came through, is that true?

Natasha: Um . . . the person who did that group *said* she was there, but I didn't feel like she was. As a matter of fact, today I was speaking aloud to my mom, saying, "I didn't feel like you were there."

John: Okay, that makes sense with what the message is, then. You did have that previous experience, but you were rationalizing that she wasn't there. My message to you is that she *was* there. I will say that if she did come through, then you got about two seconds—

Natasha: Yeah, it's true.

John: I also feel that she recognized that that might not have been . . . and this is very key Natasha . . . she might not have been ready to come through at that time, either because of the "medium" or the facilities that were given to her to do this. She might have felt like . . . *that's not my style, I'm not gonna go there.* You follow what I'm saying?

Natasha: Exactly. I wasn't comfortable with the facilities or the medium either.

John: She's telling me to tease you about the candy, the chocolate. I don't know if there's a joke about the black-and-white cookie. But there's like a black-and-white cookie, black-and-white toffee, taffy, I don't know what this is.

Natasha: There's a chocolate connection that we have.

John: She's making me feel like you'll hear from her again. Did her cancer affect her stomach?

Natasha: Not really.

John: She's showing me a tube coming out of the stomach. Something coming out of her side. Either that or she had a feeding tube in. Is that back to your dad?

Norris: My father had a feeding tube.

John: He had two "J" names?

Norris: His name was James, but people called him Jay.

John: Okay, he had two "J" names . . . that's his way of jumping back in. I guess he got a second wind and had to pop back in. [laughing]

Norris: [laughing] Good!

John: I had a big pull-back. They're pulling back their energy. Just know that they saw this as their way of coming through . . . .

I always try to make it a point to tell a sitter *everything* that comes through to me during a session, no matter how serious, silly, or confusing I think it might be. So I was kicking myself after this reading when I found out who Norris was. I looked down at the notes I'd scribbled during the session and at the recurring doodle that covered the entire first page of my notebook: *a mailbox.* During the reading, I couldn't figure out why I kept getting an image of a mailbox in my mind, and why my guides weren't showing me my usual symbol for mail—a letter. Did Norris have a mailman in the family? I meant to ask. But obviously, there were several "Mailers" in the house!

Norris's reading was the culmination of many starts and stops in the setting-up phase. Natasha was initially trying to arrange for me to read a couple for this book to show an example of a family-type reading. She had contacted Norris—whom she'd interviewed years before—in the hopes that she and her husband, the renowned author Norman Mailer, would be interested in doing a reading together. Norris was already a big fan of *Crossing Over,* but unfortunately, as she recalled with a chuckle, "My beloved husband didn't share my enthusiasm. If I was watching the show and he came into the room to watch TV, I had to turn it off. I'm not sure why he reacted that way, but he did."

So it was no surprise that Norman wasn't eager to do a reading. Natasha informed me that she was chucking the "couple" idea and setting up a one-on-one, in-person session with just the wife she'd contacted. That was fine by me, but once again fate intervened. As she was arranging the solo reading for the following week, Norris got the news that her cancer had returned. She had to go into surgery immediately and couldn't make the trip to New York for the reading. Undeterred, and certain that Norris was "meant" to get this reading, Natasha set up a post-surgery phone reading for two weeks later, when Norris would be home convalescing and the skeptical hubby would be out of town on business.

As soon as we started the reading, Norris's dad came through and validated his daughter's physical and spiritual struggle with cancer, as well as the fact that she was still in the midst of this battle. But what impressed Norris most were the details that came through about her father's own illness and the very intimate moment when he sent Norris and her mother out of the room so he could cross over.

"He sent us both from the room in a big, clear voice after not being able to speak at all for weeks," Norris recalled. "He said, 'I want you to take your mother to the cafeteria and make her eat a good breakfast. She hasn't been eating right.' I naively thought, *Wow, he's able to speak! We'll go get breakfast and then come back and have a good conversation.* He died soon after we left. As we sat in the cafeteria, my mother started to shiver and said, 'It's so cold in here.' I knew later that he had to send us away in order to be able to cross over. But hearing it during the reading made it much easier."

Norris's dad, James, talked about other family members during the reading and gave very accurate details. Norris noted, "What you said about his sister was right on the money. She was younger, but always tried to boss the family around, and especially tried to boss *him,* which he hated, although he loved her. You got that there was some difficulty with someone not being able to tell him she loved him, and that was her. She thought if she told him she loved him he'd know he was dying . . . so she would say, 'We'll see you,' when she left. She told me more than once that she regretted she didn't say 'I love you.' When I called her right after the reading, she listened with interest, but you were right again when you said that she wouldn't really believe in it."

But Norris herself found much comfort in the details of the session, especially knowing that her dad was, literally, in the room with her during the reading—as well as being with her in spirit during her cancer battles.

She recalled, "During the reading you asked, 'Do you keep his picture on your desk to the left?' In the room where I sat during the reading, I had a picture of my father on my right, which I mentioned. But later, when I went to my computer at the desk, I saw the big picture of my father on my *left,* as it has been for years!"

Another bit of "trivial" information that wowed Norris was the mention of the "rotten eggs." That message may have seemed trivial to me as I gave it, or to you as you read the transcript—but it was of vital importance to Norris. The night before the reading, she'd had a little "chat" out loud with her father and asked him to come through with a secret sign to prove it was him . . . to mention the runny eggs Benedict he'd tried for the very first time when he'd had breakfast with Norris during the publicity tour for her novel, *Windchill Summer,* three years earlier. Dad indeed came through with the "rotten" eggs, and "it was such a clear message, it totally blew me away," said Norris. "I couldn't stop laughing. There is *no way* anybody but Daddy would have mentioned the eggs!"

Mention of her dad's friend, Charlie, hit home as well. Charlie had passed away just a few months before Norris's dad. And the Lynn who dropped by to say hello, said Norris, was her own friend Mara Lynn, a former Broadway dancer and showgirl, who had paid Norris a visit to say good-bye before she passed away last year. The last few validations during the reading—her father's two "J" names, the feeding tube, and a painful tooth "disaster"— were "totally" validating for Norris. "He just wanted to make good and sure I knew it was him, but in my mind there was no question at all."

But the biggest, most dramatic validation that Dad was with her was the mention of Norris twisting her hair as we spoke on the phone that night. "It's a habit of mine, and I was doing it! So Daddy was standing there watching me. It was so comforting." The hair-twisting, and the picture of Norris's father that I mentioned earlier, are good examples of how a phone reading can really work to the sitter's benefit—when I can come through with information about an object or an action going on in the room where the sitter is while I'm hundreds of miles away.

Norris got off the phone that night determined to heed her father's encouragement to open her eyes to every wonderful moment life had to offer, and close her eyes during the dark moments. "My father mentioned a tunnel, which might have several meanings, but a new one surfaced a few weeks after the reading," Norris told me. "I had to have an MRI, which is sort of like a scary tunnel, and he'd said, 'If you close your eyes, you won't know you're in the tunnel,' so while I was in the machine, I closed my eyes and pretended I was at a John Cage concert, and it worked pretty well."

Norris waited a day or so before calling up husband Norman on his business trip to tell him about the reading. She didn't know what kind of reaction to expect from him. As it turns out, he had a good laugh about it—"He figured I'd sneak around and do it when he was out of town." Norris laughed. But once her doubtful husband got home and read a transcript of the session, even *he* was somewhat swayed. "He said, 'Well, I may not believe in all this, but I believe the man has *something*.' I haven't given up on converting my husband, who is, by the way, also spiritual in much the same way I am. He'll just have to come to it in his own time."

Speaking of timing, when it was all over I wondered why Natasha's mother had chosen Norris's reading to finally come through even though the two parents didn't know each other. I asked both if they had any thoughts on that, and did they ever. When setting up the reading, Norris had casually asked Natasha if she'd ever had a reading herself, to which Natasha replied no, but she hoped one day to have one because she really wanted her mom to come through. The two women joked on the phone that maybe Norris's relatives would be ever-so-kind enough to bring Natasha's mom through for a cameo appearance during her reading—*ha, ha, ha*. Well, it's not so funny, lemme tell ya. If I had a dime for every time someone requested something like this aloud, in jest, and then it *happened*—I'd be richer than Rockefeller . . . or even Oprah. The two parents obviously heard this appeal, got together, and made good on it.

Some of the information that didn't make sense for Norris during the session made perfect sense for Natasha, including the reference to the number 10 (her mom passed 10 years ago), the name "Chris" (her mom's last name was Christoff), and perhaps the impact related to the number 15.

Natasha's mom, Maria, had left her hometown in Macedonia during WWII when she was 15 years old, and she used to tell stories about hearing bombs exploding near her home and seeing the war close-up. The mention of the three birthdays in December was correct (Natasha, her husband, and her twin brother); and the current birthday was also on target. Natasha had called her aunt, her mom's sister, in California just before the reading to wish her happy birthday. But the writing-in-the-sky validation for my friend was the reference to chocolate. The mother and daughter shared a passion for chocolate—and many a chocolate bar—together.

But that's not the end of it. The two also share chocolate in the *afterlife* together. Like Norris's dad, Natasha's mother couldn't speak for many weeks prior to her passing because her brain tumor had affected her speech. But there was one articulate moment during that time, for about five minutes, where she spoke perfectly.

"And of all things, she asked me if I had any chocolate," Natasha recalled, "and those were the last words I ever heard her speak." In honor of those words—and of their mutual love of the stuff—Natasha has kept up a chocolate ritual with her mom. Whenever she visits Mom's gravesite, she takes a chocolate bar or a cookie and "shares" it with her mother—eating half and breaking off the other half to leave on the tombstone. Like Norris, Natasha had given Mom specific instructions at their most recent chocolate party together. With a mouth filled with an Oreo cookie, Natasha said aloud: "Mom, if you ever come through to John, mention our chocolate. . . . " And she surely did.

The reading with Norris and Natasha, just one hour before Deanna's session, was a model of an extremely smooth reading. But let's go back to Deanna for a moment. Although her reading had some bumps in the road, it was still a positive journey. In fact, Deanna was very happy with the validations she did receive after we waded through the murky parts. First and foremost, she wanted to connect with her son, Nicholas, and she felt confident that we'd done that.

"The most amazing part for me was when you told me that someone I knew or myself had lost a child . . . and that it was a son, and that his death was sudden, which it was," Deanna told me. "Nicholas had epilepsy most of his life and suffered from seizures. But the last year and a half of his life, his health had improved through medication and diet, which is something that came through in the reading. In fact, the day before he died, he was outside playing. He went to sleep and didn't wake up in the morning."

One misinterpretation that was causing confusion in the reading, we later discovered, was that Nicholas was coming through to me as if he were at Deanna's "side," like a buddy. And that affected how I was seeing all the other relationships and "levels" he was talking about.

"It's true, I've always said to people that Nicholas was like my friend and he helps me," said Deanna. Once we cleared up that misunderstanding, we were able to move on with more ease. "You began connecting with family members who had passed, and were able to say the first names of my father and grandfather and grandmother . . . which blew me away. You figured out correct illnesses and locations where people lived.

"I was also floored when you mentioned that my son was at a recent family celebration. At first I couldn't think of anything, and we let it go. But later during the reading when you said my son was mentioning a recent celebration again, this time it clicked . . . the week before I had gotten engaged. During my engagement, I was thinking about my son, and at the same time my fiancé said, 'I feel like Nick is here.' Now there's no doubt for me that my son was present to join in our celebration. And another specific point was that Nicholas died on the 20th, and his father's birthday is the 24th. So we wanted to have the funeral before the 24th because his dad didn't want to have the funeral on his birthday."

The two readings for Deanna and Norris were two entirely different experiences, and that's why I always tell people to check their expectations at the door beforehand. You must be prepared for both disappointment and surprises during a session. The process doesn't always work perfectly, or work as we think it should or want it to. But in its imperfection, it's still a supreme gift from the Other Side.

Before Deanna and I hung up, she asked me about the concept of a "visit." She said that she often feels her son around her—especially in moments when she needs help—and she feels that he comes to her aid. I told her that I had no doubt at all that her son was looking out for her. Our children on the Other Side look out for us just as much as our parents do. And the intertwining of Norris's and Natasha's readings, with the small but important details that came through—the "eggs" for Norris and the "chocolate" for Natasha—is reason enough to believe that our loved ones hear our prayers . . . and answer them.

CHAPTER SIX

Circle of Love

As my co-workers at *Crossing Over* know all too well, no one within a 100-foot radius of me when I'm in reading mode is immune to Other Side radar. The episode of the show that viewers ask me most about is the one where I did a reading for a guy named Basil (not Natasha's dad), who was the manager of the parking garage adjacent to our first studio in Manhattan. This guy wasn't even in the room, but his relatives from beyond saw that he was close enough to be pulled into the studio from outside so they could say a few words. Dozens of crew members on *Crossing Over*, including the cameramen and producers of the show, have been surprised during the taping of the show when I've zeroed in on *them* instead of members of the gallery.

Another example of a "surprise" reading happened early in 2003 when I was a guest on *Larry King Live*. Live TV is a great arena to illustrate how this process works, moment by moment. Since *Crossing Over* is taped, TV audiences don't get a chance to see the instant electricity happening the way the members of the gallery do. On this night, after chatting with Larry, we opened up the phone lines so I could give quick readings to callers watching the show. When

I do this, the phone lines are usually jammed up within seconds, and the callers wait for a long time to finally get on the air and get their two-minute connection to me and the Other Side.

This day was no different, as people called in from all over the world and the lines lit up like a pinball machine. But wouldn't you know it . . . of all times to get stuck during a reading, it happens on live television. I was on the phone with an eager caller, and he wasn't validating a word I was saying. And yet, this information was coming through to me with such clarity. *Was anyone else in the room with him?* I asked. Nope. *Was this for a relative or friend?* Nope.

The lights on the phone were blinking with dozens of callers on hold, but this energy coming through wasn't going to let me move to the next person until I finished with him first. I was starting to worry that we were in for a major delay, when out of the blackness of the studio someone spoke up. "I think it might be for me," said the voice, coming from the shadows. It was a relative of the studio makeup artist, sitting way off to the side. I didn't even know she was there, but she heard the information and knew it was for her.

I started giving her a reading, and we continued on into the commercial break and after we came back on the air. When we were through, I was able to move on to the next caller. But it just goes to show you that the Other Side doesn't take note of doors or walls . . . and it doesn't care whether you've made an appointment or not. If you're nearby, you're fair game. I don't control who comes through or when, but I do know that timing is everything for all involved—both for the energy on the Other Side and the friend or relative here. The energy coming through has to be ready to come through, and the person here has to be ready to receive the messages.

ON FEBRUARY 11, 2003, I was scheduled to read Kristin Chenoweth, a well-known Broadway performer, on *Crossing Over*. I'm a big fan of Kristin's (I will admit it, I brought one of her CDs to the studio so she could autograph it), and she and the two pals she brought with her were avid fans of the show. It's always a pleasure do a reading for people who are familiar with the process and eager and open to see it in action . . . so I was looking forward to it.

That morning I was on my way to the gym when I felt that unmistakable tingling at the back of my neck . . . an energy was trying to get my attention, and I knew from past experience that this energy must "belong" to the reading I was to do later that day. I made a mental note to myself that it felt like a husband/brother/friend vibration coming through, and I asked him to wait and come back later at the beginning of the reading.

When I walked onto the set that afternoon, I was introduced to a very bubbly Kristin and her two best friends from grad school, Denny and Erin—and, surprise, surprise, take a guess who was also with Kristin acting as her publicist? None other than our Jill! I hadn't seen Jill since Australia, so we exchanged a few *G'day, mates* and *Good on ya's* before she scooted up to the control room. Then Kristin, her friends, and I got down to the serious business of the reading.

From the start, the reading seemed to jump around a lot . . . going from Kristin to Denny to Erin and back again. But there was that one male figure who came through first, and kept coming back, who didn't connect with either of the three people in front of me. *Here we go again,* I thought. *I wonder who he belongs to?* I really wanted Kristin to have a good session, and here was this male figure coming through with all this information that no one could validate. I struggled with it for a bit and continued to deliver his messages, hoping that something would ring a bell for one of them. When it didn't, I decided that the male coming through must be for a friend of theirs not present—which, I explained to them, does happen sometimes. Just when I thought we could move forward, the voice of our director, Dana, came over the public-address system.

"John . . . it's possible that what you were saying is for someone here in the control room. . . . "

Well, well . . . the staff does it again, I chuckled to myself. And in the middle of a celebrity reading! I wondered, *Who is it this time?*

John: I have to tell you that before I even got here today I was getting an energy coming through, and since you're the only people I'm reading today, it must be for you. It was a male energy to the side—like a husband, brother, or friend. When somebody jumps out first, it's for a reason. They either don't think they're going to get my attention or they want to make it clear that *I'm the first one here!*

It's a brother figure who passed . . . and he's connected to two "J's." There has to be a "JE" or a "JL" who's still here . . . a Jenny or a Jeffrey. And there's a celebration coming up . . . an engagement or a wedding in the family. I feel like I'm outside of my state here . . . like I'm right below New York in New Jersey or Pennsylvania. I feel like his passing is subtle. It's not a long, drawn-out feeling. It's like he's here, and then he leaves. The month of May also has a connection with the family.

Connected to you, Kristin, I feel a grandmother energy that has passed. The energy is connected to the father's side . . . connected to her is a symphony of music and prayer. It's like a blend of spirituality and music going out to the masses. And I feel like she wants me to compliment you on the blend. I need to acknowledge something that happened when you were nine or ten. I don't know if it's the first time you did something in front of her? But it was major.

Kristin: It makes sense.

John: Now, I'm also supposed to talk about this male, this first male I talked about. I don't think he's related by blood to any of you, so one of you has a friend who lost a brother or husband. He's the first person who got my attention before I even got here.

There's another male to the side coming through. He wants me to acknowledge that someone's going out to the West Coast, and it's going to be fun and sun and festive and gambling, so that makes me think Las Vegas.

And there's a father figure who's passed . . . it's not with Kristin. It's a father-in-law, a father, or an uncle who's connected to the "B" name. He's the "B" name or there's a "B" connection to him . . . like Benjamin or Benny. And October is connected here as well. It could be a birthday [looking at Erin]. I believe he passed from something cardiovascular or stroke related. The passing was quick, but I do think he was ill for a while. I just don't think it was detected. I think they almost detected something two to three months prior to his passing, but it was overlooked. There's a "Michael" connection to one of the people we're talking about . . . I think Michael is here . . . and they're making me feel like someone's birthday is in April. The first person who lost a brother . . . ?

Erin: Cousin.

John: A male cousin?

Erin: Yes.

John: Do you have the out-of-state connection? And there are two "J's." No . . . someone else has the brother who passed, or you guys are connected to the person whose brother has passed.

He's kind of a smart-ass. He's making me feel like, "I said I was gonna do this, and now I'm doing this—I'm back." I don't know if someone made a statement to him knowing that you were coming here . . . saying, "You better show up today" . . . but he's joking, like, "Well, I'm *here!*" And I'm being shown the month of April and white flowers, which to me is a birthday. And they're showing it to me twice. There's got to be something two times in April. . . .

The information I'm giving at this point just isn't ringing a bell with any of the sitters. I was about to repeat it all again, when Dana interrupts me from the control room to let me know that the "smart-ass" most likely belongs to someone in there. He asks if that person should come out and do the reading face-to-face, but I said no. I figured I could probably get their reading done and over with quicker if I didn't know who it was. And while I wanted to honor this person and their loved one on the Other Side, I was also anxious to continue with Kristin's reading.

We arranged for Doug, the stage manager, to give me yes/no answers given to him through his earpiece from the mystery sitter in the control room. It got a little confusing at times, as relatives and names started to overlap between the many sitters in classic "me, too" fashion.

Control room: You can ask questions, and we'll pass them on.

John (repeating): There's a connection to a brother or husband who had passed. There's a connection to two "J" names. There's an engagement or special announcement I'm feeling very excited about. I think this is happening within the year. And there's a connection to April as a birthday. The passing of this male isn't long ago . . . maybe two or three years. Do you understand that?

Control room: Yep.

John: There's a "me, too" thing here. One male figure to the side is connected to a Michael, and one wants me to acknowledge two nephews or two kids. And I think I'm supposed to say the name "Jeffrey." Is there a Jeff connected to you?

Erin: Jeff is my cousin who passed, and his brother is Mark, not Michael.

John: Mark might be the "MK"-sounding name I was getting. I get Michael, Mark, Mickey, names with strong "MK" sounds, the same way.

Control room: That works in here, too, John.

John: I knew I was going to get a "me, too." I have dueling brother/husband figures here. [To Erin]: Mark is your cousin? Is the Mark or Mike connected to the control room?

Then Doug, the stage manager, slips up. Or at least I think he does. He tells me he's going to check that last "Mark" validation in the control room "with him." I give Doug a dirty look. He just gave away that it was a man I was reading! And did he mean he was going to check with "Mark"? We have a "Mark" in the control room, so this must be for him, since his name was being thrown around. This must be for Mark, I'm thinking. Yep, I thought for sure it was . . . until . . .

Control room: No, the "Mark" doesn't make sense in here.

John: I want to be clear that the "MK" name is Mark. His mom is still here?

Erin: Yes.

John: You have his photo in your house, right?

Erin: I do . . . at home I do.

John: Is there snow in the background of the photo?

Erin: There might be . . . he visited us in Michigan during the winter.

John: I need to bring up the snow picture . . . does that make sense for the control room?

Control room: No.

John: Okay, I need to bring up some kind of . . . it looks like a ski lodge. There's a woodsy feeling. And . . . he might be to the side, but would you see him as older?

Erin: A little.

John: Is Jeff older than he is?

Erin: Yes.

John: Just let Jeff know he came through. Tell Jeff he sees the fact that he moved. With your cousin Mark, the spiritual event I'm getting that's coming up is more in connection with a child—as if a child is christened or had a confirmation.

Connected to the control room, I get an engagement, a wedding. And I'm seeing my cousin's birthday, August 19th, so there must be an August 19th connection in the control room?

Control room: Yes, August 20th.

John: The brother figure has someone who passed in a vehicle accident with him . . . unless that's how he passed.

There's a vehicle impact that takes place. Is this for the control room?

Control room: No.

Erin: Mark had a landscaping accident.

John: It has to be an impact. I feel like I'm being impacted.

Erin: No.

John: I need to be clear. Connected to the person in the control room, someone passes in a vehicle accident. They're not driving or responsible for this, but I feel like I'm supposed to say Marilyn or Mabel or Marabel, which is connected to this in some way. Some sort of unique "M" name.

Whoever passes with the impact . . . there's like a misprint in an obituary. Like the cause of how they passed was wrong, was incorrect. But it was rectified. But a big deal wasn't made about it.

The person with the impact isn't related by blood with the brother. The brother wants to bring this person through and acknowledge that there's some type of split happening in that family, where someone else in that family has passed or has left . . . or passed . . . an older male. The Jeffrey is connected to the control room, too, right?

Living?

Control room: Yes.

John: The brother figure wants me to say that people need to talk about this passing. It needs to be discussed. It's a sad passing, but they don't want to upset someone, so they don't talk about it. The guy is making me feel like *I want to be talked about!* I'm not getting that from your Mark [looking at Erin]. I'm getting it from the other energy who was the first one to get my attention.

I get the feeling that they're teasing that they could do this anytime. Like here at work when I'm walking down the hall and I can get pulled into an office. . . . "Oh, by the way, I've got your brother figure coming through." But they waited until I cannot *not* pay attention. For some reason, they chose today's date to do this. There must be something significant about the date today for the family.

I'm also supposed to acknowledge that Richard or Robert has to be connected to them as well. The "R" name . . . that's for the control room.

Control room: Not so far.

John: Absolutely, there's a Rick or Rich . . . a male "R" name connected to him. There's also a brain-tumor connection. This is for the control room as well. . . .

Control room: Yes . . . there's a Rick who died of a brain tumor.

John: Connected to the male figure to the side?

Control room: Yes, it is.

John: Okay, this guy is a *pain in the butt!* [laughing] I'm supposed to tease about eating pretzels. Right at this second, are they eating pretzels or something? If not, is there some kind of joke about the pretzels?

Control room: Not eating pretzels at this moment.

John: Then there has to be a pretzel reference that I feel has to be a joke. Is Dad there, too? Dad must be passed.

Control room: Yes.

John: And Dad passed *before* him. Dad wants to acknowledge the grandchildren. I also need to acknowledge four or five kids in the family. There's a reference to someone who's known for having issues with alcohol. And there's a reference to some sort of disconnect . . . it's either with the baby of the family, or the "one" . . . like if there are four boys and one girl, it's the girl. It's like they had to make their own space, and I need to compliment them on what they did. They came into their own by doing that, but never lost sight of the family at the same time. Does that make sense?

Control room: Yes, it does.

John: Mom has to have a brother as well there, besides Dad. There's got to be a brother or a brother-in-law for Mom there. It could also be a close family friend who lost a husband, but I feel it's connected to Mom.

Control room: Yes.

John: The father figure needs the family to know he's around. There's a wedding or engagement or birth of a child coming up . . . a family event that both the father and younger male want the family to know—this is really important that they're going to be there for this. The family needs to hear this. The brother is pushing the father figure out of the way, like, okay, you're done and now I'm back! And I need to talk about being on TV. This guy is such a ham. There's a total *I'm-messing-with-you* feeling . . .

He wants me to tease you about the shoes. [To Kristin]: Were you not going to wear those shoes today?

Kristin: Me? I wasn't . . . no, I wasn't!

John: Why would this person's brother be talking about your shoes? They're showing me fuchsia . . . hot pink. You don't have anything pink on except your lipstick.

Kristin: I had a hot pink, fuchsia heart on last night.

John: Well, they were with you last night then. Why this . . . this doesn't make any sense. But it's like the person in the control room, their brother, wants me to acknowledge you were wearing whatever this is. I don't understand this. It has to be a conversation you had—

Control room: John, this *does* make sense in here.

John: It *does?*

Control room: They were together last night.

Okay, so now I'm totally, *totally* confused. Why the heck would someone in my control room be hanging out with Kristin Chenoweth? There's just no way . . . this didn't make sense. I'm racking my brain trying to figure out what lucky guy had a hot date with Kristin the night before . . . and then it hit me. This was not for Mark or any other man—or woman, for that matter—on *Crossing Over.* This could only be for someone who knew Kristin well and who was with her last night at whatever glittery affair she was attending, and who was also in the control room today. . . .

I was baffled and couldn't figure it out (self-psychic amnesia?) when Doug, the stage manager, finally leaned over and let me in on the secret. "John, it's JILL!" I was shocked.

> **John** (pause): What? This is for *Jill?!*
> **Kristin:** Yes!

I was stunned—and totally excited. And I had to stop for a second and take a breath. Jill had totally "pulled a Natasha" and had purposely kept details of her family and their history from me. And now here they were, making an appearance. My heart just melted, and I couldn't stop smiling at the thought of Jill up there getting her own reading in secret. Especially after she'd watched me do hundreds of readings, and never once did anything come through for her. As soon as we finished up with Jill's relative coming through, I was able to finish Kristin's reading.

> **John** (to Kristin): On your dad's side, there's this woman—I don't know if you knew her in life, but I feel she's very strongly tethered to the energy of what you do. Is there anyone on your dad's side who used to do what you do?
> **Kristin:** I'm not sure.
> **John:** I would love for you to find out. Because there's such a strong feeling of "she's following in my footsteps." Like someone else did this.
> **Kristin:** I've wondered about that.
> **John:** There had to be, in your development, some type of overwhelming standing ovation. Like you got out in front of thousands of people at a very young age. But it's spiritual to me . . . like you were asked to sing in church.
> **Kristin:** I did—it was in front of 10,000 people when I was nine or ten.
> **John:** That event was a pivotal experience. You already had a taste early on of what if feels like to be known and appreciated. And you're now blending the two worlds

again. What you did in front of 10,000 people, you're now moving it forward.

Kristin: My next album will be "Faith and Inspiration."

John: Remember how Natalie Cole did the Nat King Cole overlay? Either you're doing an overlay or doing a duet with yourself. As if there were two separate Kristins singing . . . there are two of you. And I'm supposed to tell you that what's not being handed to you today on a professional level probably isn't going to happen for another three years. But it's a positive, not a negative. Something you're going to do will be different from what you're known for, and you'll go in a different direction. Maybe it's publishing or writing music . . . something different, an adjunct, another outlet of the same thing. There's something about going to Europe. I don't know if maybe you're planning to go to Vienna? There's a large international feeling, and you'll be asked to sing in a different language or do something different from what I know you as doing. . . .

And, the pull you already have in your leg? Stay on top of it. It's always a warning, so be careful. This is muscle related; it feels like you had a tear. Normally, it wouldn't be a problem, but if you do something like this, it will be an issue.

Now . . . did you get the cat yet? They want to know if you got the cat yet.

Kristin: I'm giving him my cat! [She points to Denny.]

John: These are the trivial little things to show you they know what's going on.

They're pulling their energy back. . . .

When the reading was over, we all had a laugh at how Jill's brother had "messed with me," as he put it—and I was amazed and more than a bit freaked out at how the reading for Jill had come about.

"Boom, boom, *boom*—you had everything right," Jill said as she ran down from the control room excitedly listing off the validations: "My dad and my brother have both passed. I'm from Pennsylvania, and you said that. The "JE" and the "JL" . . . I'm Jill, my brother is Jeff, and my brother who passed is Joe. His birthday is August 20th, and he died in May . . . you said there was a May connection . . . and the two-year anniversary is coming up . . . and it was a sudden passing, like you said.

"My mother had talked to him the day before, and he said he wasn't feeling well, and he said he was going to go to sleep and we didn't hear from him for two days . . . and he had passed in his apartment of a heart problem. He was here one day, gone the next. And then you said April for a birthday . . . my birthday is April. You called my brother a ham, and it's true . . . he used to tease me all the time like the way *you* tease me. And then last night, with the pink heart . . . we were laughing because Kristin was going to wear something with a pink, fuchsia heart on it, and we were like; wear it . . . don't wear it . . . wear it . . . don't wear it . . . take it off . . . put it on . . . I never told you any of this stuff, and you nailed it. Except . . . I don't know what the pretzel thing is. . . . "

It was such a rush of emotion and elation that I saw coming out of my friend, and I was so happy that her family had come through for her. And once again, I was amazed at the timing of it all. Why didn't her family come through earlier, during all of our business trips and seminars and lunches and long drives in the car?

"I guess, for whatever reason, it had to take that long—maybe so I could understand the process better," Jill told me. After she explained more about her family, I realized that there was more of a "timing" thing happening than I thought. Remember when I told you earlier that when I first met Jill I felt that there was an important reason she needed to be connected with this work?

Well, when her friend and client Aaliyah died in that plane crash, I thought that was the reason she would be questioning mortality. But I had no idea that the first time I had called her for a meeting, it was almost to the day of her brother's death.

"Actually, that's another strange story," Jill told me. "You called me the first or second day after he passed, and I pretty much freaked out because I was like, why is he calling me *now?* What does he know?"

It wasn't until over a year later in conversation when she casually mentioned that she'd lost a brother. I thought it was odd that she'd never mentioned it before, and I asked her why she hadn't.

"John, you *always* tell me not to tell a medium *any* information," she laughed, "and if he ever showed up, I'd want to know I hadn't told you *anything* about it." And for that reason, we dropped the subject right away without her telling me any more. I was shocked at how professional she'd been—never taking the opportunity as we worked together to try to arrange a reading for herself or anyone in her family.

At least she didn't try to arrange it *with me*. Jill had had a little chat with her brother before Kristin's reading. "The other day, I said to my brother out loud, 'By the way . . . if you are *ever* going to come through, why don't you come through on Tuesday when I'm going to be in the studio? Wouldn't that be funny? Ha, ha!' But I still didn't think it would happen. When I was in the greenroom, they wanted me to sign the release form in case I was read, and I told them, 'Look, I don't need to sign the form. I'm with John all the time! Believe me, I'm not going to be read. I talk to him a hundred times a day, and *no one ever comes through for me.*'"

But let me reiterate: People come through in their own time and in their own mysterious ways. Kristin had to be there that day so that Jill's brother and father could come through.

"And I was glad it was me," piped up Kristin, who was thrilled about her own messages as well. I myself was most curious about Kristin's "international" singing reference and asked her what that was all about.

"I went to London this summer and sang, but I sing in other languages, too," she explained. "I've done *Phantom* in German— in Germany. And I was asked while I was in London to come back to do an international festival this summer and sing more of a religious type of music. My great-aunt Inez would always encourage me and come to church and hear me sing, so that's who I think came through on my father's side.

"I was asked to sing at the Southern Baptist Convention in Oklahoma in front of 10,000 people when I was nine or ten. It was huge.

When you said it was 'spiritually based,' it was so true, and my aunt was a part of that. It was a real turning point in my life and a big deal. You nailed that!

"Being a Christian, I know a lot of people don't look at this stuff as being 'of God.' But I believe that people who leave us are with us. For me, personally, the big freak-out moment was when you said I would be doing a 'blending' of what I did with a more spiritual aspect. That definitely hit home because I'm working on my next album with Sony Classical, titled 'Faith and Inspiration.' Then when you asked if I was wearing fuchsia or pink, that cracked me up. Last night I was at the movie premiere for *The Music Man,* and I had a big pink fuchsia heart on, and there was a big discussion about what to wear and what shoes to wear. I wanted to wear these because they're more comfortable, but Jill was like, 'You have to wear the dressy boots!'

"Jill was really adamant about what I wore last night, and that's why I'm laughing . . . because her brother was teasing about it. We didn't know Jill was in the control room during the reading, so we didn't think any of this had a connection to her, and all of a sudden, it hit us like a lightbulb. And then you asked about the pull in my leg? I have a really bad hamstring injury from my high school cheerleading days, and it bothers me still."

I NEVER TIRE OF WATCHING how hard the Other Side works to get their messages through to us, and I'm still amazed after all these years at their elaborate methods. In this case, Kristin's family acted as a link for opening for Jill's family to come through in such a way that I wouldn't know it was for her—thereby protecting the integrity of the experience, just as Jill had hoped.

When someone's getting a reading and they bring through family for a friend, I call that the widening of the "circle of love." And Kristin's circle opened up to include our friend Jill.

To repeat once more, the Other Side comes through to us when they're ready . . . but more important, when *we're* ready. Jill waited a year and a half for her family to show up, but they didn't arrive until all the elements were right. I can't control who comes through, and neither can you. It's up to them, and they know best.

"My mother was always saying to me, 'You work with John Edward. I don't understand why you can't just ask him to do a reading!'" Jill told me afterwards. "She didn't understand why you weren't having conversations with my brother all the time. And I told her, 'Mom . . . it doesn't work that way. If it's meant to be, it will happen. When the time is right, it will just happen.'"

CHAPTER SEVEN

Teachers

PSYCHIC PUBERTY

I HAD MY FIRST ENCOUNTER with psychic work in 1985 when I attempted to debunk a woman named Lydia Clar, who arrived at my home one afternoon to do readings for my mother and a bunch of other eager relatives. I, too, had my very first reading that day—reluctantly. I didn't believe in that kind of silly stuff, but I went along with it, at my cousin's urging, to prove that this woman was a fraud. But it was at that initial reading, at age 15, when I was told that I'd someday be an internationally known psychic, lecture around the world, and write numerous books on the subject of psychic phenomena. Ha! I laughed at this, thinking, *How psychic could this woman be if she can't even pick up that I think she's full of s—t?*

Lydia foresaw my career as a psychic medium 16 years before it began. And what did she get in return? About $35 and a whole lot of attitude from me. In life, there are many signposts and teachers along the way. Lydia, I didn't know it at the time, was the first person who pointed me in the right direction. As they say, when the student is ready, the teacher will appear. But I wasn't quite ready . . . yet.

One of my most important teachers was a stranger who was to become one of my best friends. My previous book, *CROSSING OVER: The Stories Behind the Stories*, is dedicated to the memory and energy of a psychic medium and astrologer named Shelley Peck, who was my dearest pal.

I want to talk about Shelley here for many reasons. One primary reason is because she and I shared much of the same philosophy and thoughts about our work, and even worked in a similar style. At times, it was downright shocking to us how alike we were. After events we did together, we'd talk for hours and compare the "Hey, me, toos" we shared.

I'm sure you'd be surprised to know that Shelley was almost 30 years older than I. One of the funniest moments in our friendship was when I'd call Shelley's home on a weeknight and one of her three kids would answer the phone. They were all around my age, but I'd be asking them if their mom could "come out and play." It was something her husband, Marvin, had to shake his head at. So, how did the Universe arrange for Shelley and me to meet?

After my reading with Lydia Clar that day in my house, I needed to know how she was able to do it. I figured that there had to be something to this psychic stuff because she was extremely accurate in my session, as well as with my other relatives who were read that day. I broke up her reading into three parts.

One part was the "You're going to be a famous psychic" part, where I had to restrain myself from laughing out loud right in her very serious face. Another section was where she came up with a bunch of specific information about my life that was right on target—the classes I was taking and how I was doing in them, the teachers I had, and the girls I had crushes on. Okay, could she actually have some ability? I rationalized most of what she said as stuff that would apply to any hormonally charged teenage boy.

Then came the last part, which made me sit up and take notice. Lydia brought up a private situation in my life that nobody—not even my family—knew about. She gave me details about a girl I liked, mentioned a few names related to this girl, and even predicted the outcome of the romance. After the session, my head was spinning as I tried to poke holes in the reading, but I couldn't do it. I felt out of control and even a bit . . . violated. That might sound absurd, but that's the feeling you sometimes get from a good reading when a stranger "exposes" your private life out loud like a grocery list is being read. In case you've ever had that experience, you should know that it's normal to feel that way.

Lydia didn't go out of her way to try to "teach" me anything that day. She was there to set me on course. After making her startling pronouncements, she didn't even recommend a book I should read on the topic of psychic phenomena. I think back to that reading and consider her more like the first "gardener" of my uncultivated psychic soil. She planted the seeds, and grow they did—my interest was like a weed spreading out of control.

I started out at the library with a few books. Soon, I was reading anything I could get my hands on that was written about parapsychology or metaphysics. Like many of you reading this right now, I had a lot of questions, such as: *What's it all about?* and *How does it work?* Soon, I was reading books on the deeper meanings of tarot cards during English class instead of focusing on *A Tale of Two Cities* or *Lord of the Flies*—much to my teacher's chagrin.

It was then that I realized I needed professional help. No, I don't mean a therapist who would examine me and dissect my inner psyche. I needed someone who actually did psychic work to explain it and help guide me through it. And since I was 15 and didn't have a driver's license yet, I needed that person to live close by (Lydia Clar lived in New Jersey, a whole other state). And I needed this person pronto. I mean, I was told that I had these "powers" and these highly evolved guides who were ready to work with me—words that sounded straight out of Yoda's mouth in the Jedi training camp. Great! I have these abilities? Where are the instructions? It wasn't like I could wiggle my nose or cross my arms like in *Bewitched* and blink up a prediction . . . or someone's grandpa from the Other Side.

The best analogy I can give you is that Lydia told me I can speak this "other language"—think of it as the language of energy. And like any other language, you had to develop an understanding and command of it. This is exactly what psychic development felt like for me—learning the language of a whole new world. But until I could find the proper teacher to tutor me, I continued to teach myself by reading and putting into practice anything I learned.

By the time I was 16, I was dabbling in readings of my own, and I'd met with moderate success. I'd started to meditate regularly, had taught myself how to read playing cards from a book, and was developing skills in psychometry—the reading of a person's energy while holding something that belongs to them—such as a watch or a ring. Soon, I was able to tell people details about their life, job, relationships, and past . . . and also make predictions that would come true a few days into the future. It felt like I was tapping in to a whole new reservoir of awareness. Of course, if I was to compare my abilities then to now, it's like the difference between a drip from a leaky faucet and Niagara Falls.

WHERE TO FIND A PSYCHIC TEACHER? The Yellow Pages, of course. . . .

Although I was experiencing moderate success, I knew there was so much more I needed to learn. Desperate to find someone—anyone—to guide me, I turned to the only resource I could think of—the phone book. I'm not kidding. I let my fingers do the walking and looked under "P" for psychic. There were only a few listings, and most of them were for the storefront, neon-palm-glowing-in-the-window types. You know, the ones that tell some poor, gullible soul they have a curse on them and it will cost $5,000 to make it go away. If you ever come across a scam like this, do yourself and everyone else a favor—call the police and turn that wacko in, because that's called fraud.

My mother had an experience with a woman like this whom I nicknamed "Madame Assola" (get it?). This woman told Mom that her marriage was really bad because there was a dark cloud looming over her head that had followed her since the day she was born . . . and if my mother didn't give her $1,000 per month to light candles and pray for her, the curse could be passed down to her children.

My mom, psychic junkie that she was, wasn't stupid. She politely ended the session by saying, "Thank you for your time, but I will light my own candles in church," and left. When she related this story to me as a young boy, I will admit that I thought about the many arguments she and my dad had, and I asked her if that black cloud was something I'd inherited. My mom calmed my fears and assured me that as long as you have a strong faith in God and surround yourself in prayer, no dark clouds would be on your back—words I still believe.

Characters like that manipulating fortune-teller and any of the 1-900-dial-the-dead psychic hotlines make me sick, because they prey on trusting people in a vulnerable condition. They're why I always say it's really important to have skeptics out there to raise the "opposing views" on the subject matter. These skeptics sometimes group me in the same category with the swindlers, which I don't particularly like, but nevertheless, I still appreciate their value.

So back to my search for guidance: I flipped through the Yellow Pages and came across a listing for the Astrological Institute of Integrated Studies (AIIS) which, at the time, was located in Bayshore, Long Island, and run by a husband-and-wife team, John Maerz and Sandy Anastasi. The first thing I did was to arrange to have a reading with Sandy, who was the resident psychic. Yes, I was looking to develop the skills Lydia said I was capable of, but I wanted to check out the psychic first. This would be like going to a gym and checking out the trainers, or going to a school and sizing up the teachers.

The only snag in this plan was my mother. The psychic junkie herself didn't want me venturing into fresh, new territory all alone. I couldn't figure out if she didn't want to miss out on a good reading opportunity or if this was genuine parental concern. I personally think it was a little bit of both. She insisted that we make two appointments with the psychic, and, because she was the "Grand Dame of Readings," she had to go first. Just in case Sandy was a nut job, she would protect me, her little cub, from the psychic predator.

On the day of the reading, as I waited out in the hallway, my mom emerged from the room and gave me "The Look," which meant that not only was Sandy very good, but I was next. Once in the room, Sandy immediately picked up on my abilities and then followed through with a spectacular reading. When it was over, we discussed the classes I should take for my new psychic school curriculum. As I was still in high school, I signed up for weekly sessions on Saturday mornings. My mother was ecstatic. Some mothers want their sons to be doctors. My mom? She couldn't believe her luck: Her son was going to psychic school. She envisioned a lifetime of free readings spread out before her.

I signed on for Basic Tarot with Sandy and Basic Numerology with John. I had made it through about half of Sandy's Psychic Development One class before she politely kicked me out. She was worried that I'd make the other students feel slow because of my above-average abilities. I remember her joking around, calling me "the up-and-coming Merlin."

My studies at AIIS helped me establish a good foundation that's evident in my work today. Recently, Sandy sent me her current Basic Development book, and I flipped through it, surprised by how similar her style of teaching is to the way I conduct my workshops on developing psychic skills. I e-mailed Sandy and asked how she thought that was possible—did we possess the same guides? She was polite in her response, reminding me that I was indeed her student at one time!

Instead of accusing me of "stealing" her style, Sandy took my nod to her teachings as a compliment—glad that I was able to learn from her and use it as a basis for my own work. Sandy and John— who still help others develop their psychic abilities and now run Starchild Books in Port Charlotte, Florida—were two of my earliest, most influential teachers.

PSYCHIC FRIENDS NETWORK

DURING ONE OF MY FIRST TAROT CLASSES, held in the basement of John and Sandy's Bayshore, Long Island, home, I noticed a list of recommended Long Island psychics pinned to the wall. One person on the list, Shelley Peck, was in the same phone exchange as me.

What? There was a psychic living in the Glen Cove area and my mother didn't know her?

I jotted the number down and telephoned Shelley that afternoon when I got home. She picked up the phone at 4:30 P.M. . . . and we hung up at 7 P.M., after a nearly three-hour intense chat. We had an amazing and instantaneous connection, so I booked an appointment with her for the following week. She was fully booked for months, but because she, too, felt a connection to the voice on the other end of the phone line, she squeezed me in on her day off.

That day could not have come soon enough for me. My mom's brother, Uncle Joey, went with me to make sure his 16-year-old nephew wasn't going to be taken in by some crystal-ball-wielding wacko. I will never forget our first meeting. Shelley opened the door, looked at my Uncle Joey, then at me, and extended her hand out to Uncle Joey.

"John? Very nice to meet you. . . . " And I thought, *This is the psychic? She didn't even know who I was!*

I jumped into the conversation: "No, no . . . Shelley, it's me . . . I'm John."

She looked at me and blurted out, "You're a kid! I had a three-hour conversation about metaphysics with a kid?" and she started to laugh. "Come on in and let's talk . . . but I'm not reading you . . . you're way too young," and she shook her head, laughing at herself.

I soon found that Shelley had this very down-to-earth, matter-of- fact, good ol' New York way about her. In later years, sitting in more Long Island diners that I can count, we often laughed about that first meeting. After every house party or psychic fair we did together, we'd make a beeline to nourish the body after the soul had been fed—hamburger deluxes for me, Chinese roast pork sandwiches for her . . . and make it heavy on the duck sauce, please, or "I'll send you back for more!"

Every Sunday, the psychic fair where Shelley and I worked would be in a different location on Long Island. One particular Sunday it was to be in Port Jefferson—-about an hour and 15 minutes from where we lived. We were early, and neither of us had eaten breakfast, so we were starved. We also both realized at the same time that we'd left our wallets at home. At least I had a full tank of gas, thanks to my father instilling that rule in me early on.

But we were lucky that morning, as I happened to be driving a new car at the time—well, a new *used* car—a Dodge Charger that I nicknamed the Old Alfer (after the furry alien on the TV show *Alf*. I always saw Alf as an acerbic cross between Don Rickles and an anteater). There's that tradition you might have heard about, where, when you get a new car, your friends and family throw fistfuls of change in the back seat for luck. Well, picture this scene: Outside the hotel where the psychic seminar was to be held, where people were already lining up for hours to book appointments with Shelley and me, where were we—these two dynamic psychics? We were on our hands and knees digging our fingers between the seat cushions and scrounging change off the floor of my car, trying to scrape together enough for a cheeseburger at McDonald's.

We shared a burger and fries that morning—which led to 17 years of friendship—where we shared everything about our families and professional experiences, even though we didn't belong to the same generation.

As we worked together over the years, we discovered that there were distinct similarities in how we conducted our readings. For us, it was all in the details. One night we were both booked for a group reading, and I was looking forward, as always, to watching Shelley work. During the reading, I made a connection with one participant's relative and was able to discern a very unusual combination of illnesses that he had passed from—a very specific cardiac condition and a rare blood disease.

Shelley couldn't control herself—she was so impressed that she blurted out, "Oh my God . . . how in God's name did you get that?!" It was my background working in the health-care field as a phlebotomist (a lab blood technician) that had really increased my awareness of medical issues.

Not five minutes later, Shelley was giving information to this same woman . . . details about the small town in Prussia that her family had come from. Shelley looked over at me and saw my jaw hanging close to the floor in amazement that she was relaying information about a country that no longer existed. And with this quiet confidence, she smiled, winked at me, and explained: "I majored in geography. "

Everyone laughed that night as they witnessed the chemistry between us. Shelley and I worked together often, and just like co-workers at any job, we'd vent to one another about clients. Yes, I will admit, every once in a while (just like in any other profession), a sitter would walk through our door who wasn't especially likable. Either they'd arrive with a whole lot of attitude that I'd have to deal with before we even got started, or they'd just be completely unappreciative of the process throughout the entire reading. Sometimes, as a medium, you're talking to the dead person on the Other Side and wondering why the heck they'd even *want* to talk to this living person sitting in front of you.

Another favorite evening for us that will live forever in our shared history was the night of the "perhaps lady." Shelley invited me to her home in Roslyn, Long Island, for a group she was reading, and I brought my aunt Roseann, "Big Ro," with me. We sat on Shelley's U-shaped sofa with a dozen others as everyone waited for Shelley to bring through their loved ones. To everyone's dismay, Shelley spent a good portion of the night locked in on one woman who'd lost her husband. What made it dismal was that this woman who was hogging the reading was a hardcore cynic.

"Your husband has passed . . . yes?" Shelley directed the statement to the woman sitting next to my aunt. The woman said nothing and just stared at Shelley as if she hadn't spoken to her.

"Ma'am, I'm talking to you," Shelley said, a bit louder. "Your husband is here . . . he's the man with the colon cancer?"

"Puuuurhaaaps . . . " was the answer.

"He's telling me he's been gone for the last five years . . . "

"Puuuurhaaaps . . . " was the answer.

Shelley went on with this woman, reciting solid facts coming from this deceased husband, and every incredible piece of information she brought through was received with this sing-song

"Puuuurhaaaps." After nearly an hour of this, the other people in the room were rolling their eyes and shaking their heads. Her husband was working so hard at coming through, but instead of acknowledging the information, she was responding with all this "perhaps" crap. Then came the breaking point.

"He's telling me that there's a major orange connection," Shelley continued, " . . . and to me, I think it's the orange groves in Florida . . . but I feel it's work related in some way."

Of course, we all silently mouthed with her: *"Perhaps."*

Shelley just lost it. "Look . . . either this does or does not make sense to you. *You either do or don't understand what I'm telling you . . . YES OR NO?!"*

Finally, the one-word woman spoke. "Well . . . I don't know if I'm reaching to make this fit . . . but my husband was affiliated with orange and vitamin C products, which were all derivatives of the orange groves in Florida . . . but I'm not sure if that's it. . . . "

Shelley just stared at her, speechless. And then got the biggest laugh of the night when she answered: "Perhaps!"

A PAIN IN THE BUTT

WHEN MY MOM WAS DIAGNOSED WITH CANCER, Shelley would come to the hospital with me to see her. My mom would always perk up when she saw Shelley because she had a great respect for her and knew how much I respected her as well. On one of those visits, I remember telling Shelley as we walked through the parking lot of Syosset Hospital—one of the five or six hospitals my mom frequented from April 1989 to October 1989—that when I was a child, I used to tell my mom that if smoking ever kills her, I'd refuse to go the funeral. I was forever trying to get her to quit, and I remember making this funeral threat at least a hundred times—starting from the time I was in first grade and was taught about the dangers of cigarettes. But my mom would just shrug it off.

So now, it was indeed lung cancer that she was suffering from, and I guess you could say I was a bit high-strung during this time, with so many mixed emotions about it. I was 19 years old, and I was scared and angry. I realized the gravity of the situation, and I psychically "knew" the outcome. But at the same time, I was praying for a miracle like anybody else would whose loved one was dying of cancer.

But what happened next was like a scene straight out of a soap opera. I'd just finished telling Shelley about my childhood funeral vow as we made our way up to see my mother. The elevator doors opened, and Shelley and I walked out onto my mother's floor, down the hall, toward the lounge area. And there, sitting next to a half-open window, was my mother, in a wheelchair, *smoking*.

My father, Little Ro, and Big Ro were there . . . but I didn't know which one of them was her willing cigarette accomplice. It didn't matter. I had a complete meltdown and went ballistic. I'd love to recount for you exactly what I said, but all I remember is screaming like a lunatic. I guess that everything I was holding in—my fear of losing my mom and my hatred for smoking, the evil villain that was taking her—erupted from within. Shelley grabbed me and pushed me out of the lounge and back into the hall, but I was totally out of control.

My father stepped out of the lounge to try to calm me down, but he was about four feet away from me when I realized that *he* was the one who'd given Mom the cancer stick she was smoking. Even in my hysteria, I had the ability to process what brand of cigarette she was smoking—both Roseanns only smoked Parliament white tips . . . *he* smoked the orange Marlboros . . . and mom was smoking the *orange* one.

I felt betrayed by both of them. Back in the lounge, my mom got upset, started to cry, and was apologizing to me . . . but I didn't want to hear any of that. I was outraged and hurt that she would be smoking, and I saw it as a betrayal—like she was cheating on me and the rest of the family with her illicit nicotine. I wasn't thinking logically at the time that whatever damage the smoking was going to do to her was already done. I was just a kid, crazy and blinded with anger.

What happened next, nobody expected. *WHACK!* Shelley slapped me hard across the face in the hallway. And I assure you—she didn't hold back.

"This is not about one cigarette . . . you know that!" She shook me. "Don't make your mom feel any worse than she already does. I'm sorry I had to slap you . . . but . . . "

I was a bit stunned, but not too dazed to notice my father getting all riled up that this strange, small, blonde woman had the audacity to slap his son around—and in front of him, no less. Shelley didn't really have a fondness for my father, and she completely ignored the fact that he was standing there. She excused herself from me, walked right past my dad, went over to my mom, and told her not to worry about me—Shelley would calm me down and bring me back in to see her in a bit. Later, as we left the hospital, I burst out laughing at the whole scenario.

"Do you realize that you slapped me pretty damn hard?!" I asked her.

"Yes, I do. But I had to do something to get your attention. I think I *got* your attention, didn't I?"

"Oh . . . you got my attention all right."

Then, as we walked toward my car, Shelley pulled out a cigarette from her purse like nothing had just happened and started to light it up. I stopped dead in my tracks and looked at her. *"Are you kidding me?!"*

"I'm quitting . . . I'm quitting . . . I know . . . don't say it . . . you want to smack *me* now, right?"

Right. Maybe I should have.

MY MOTHER CROSSED ON OCTOBER 5, 1989, at 3:54 A.M. I didn't have to call Shelley to tell her my mother had officially left this world. Mom did it for me. Around ten o'clock that morning, before I had a chance to call her, Shelley phoned me to extend her condolences. To some of you this might sound strange, but for us it wasn't . . . we had that type of connection.

I didn't have to ask how she knew—I assumed that her guides had told her. But in this case, I was wrong—my *mom* had told her.

I was lying on my bed when the phone rang and Shelley asked how I was holding up. I was kind of numb, but was mentally preparing myself to get ready for a family wedding two days later, in which I was part of the bridal party. It was my mom's wish that if anything happened to her, her nephew's wedding would go on as planned, and I was instructed to make sure that her family didn't use her death as an excuse to bail out.

When Shelley called me that morning, I was trying to figure out just how to accomplish this.

"John," she said excitedly, "I have all these messages for you!"

We knew so many of the same people from our seminars that I figured she had condolences for me from our colleagues. Not exactly. Shelley had pages and pages of notes that had come directly from my mother, she said, that morning. It seemed that my mom had barely crossed over, and already she was a force to be reckoned with on the Other Side! After being sick for so many months, I'm sure that she desperately wanted me to know she was okay as soon as she was able. But was I able to hear this now?

"Your mom wanted me to tell you," Shelley began, "that she appreciates what everybody did for her and that— "

"*Whoa . . . stop! Wait a minute!*" I interrupted, mid-sentence. "I don't know if I want to hear this yet." Remember what I said earlier about waiting a certain amount of time after a loved one's passing before seeking out a medium? Well, it was true for me, too. I was only human, and I didn't feel ready. At that moment, I wasn't a psychic—I was a son who had lost his mother and was in the initial, shocking stages of mourning.

Shelley had no patience for that.

"John, I know how difficult this is," she said firmly, "but I also know how hard your mother worked to get these messages through to me to let you know that she's all right. *So I know that you're gonna get your ass up outta bed and get a piece of paper and a pen and write all this stuff down,* because I *also* know that I didn't work my butt off at seven o'clock this morning doing this for someone *who's not going to appreciate everyone's efforts . . . right?!*"

I never told her this, but at that moment she was downright getting on my nerves.

There I was, indulging in a well-deserved moment of wallowing, and that's all I wanted to do! The invitations for the pity party were out, and I was going to be the guest of honor. But my mother and Shelley wouldn't be RSVP-ing for that kind of get-together, Shelley informed me. So I dragged myself off the bed, fetched a pen and paper, and dutifully began writing.

"There's something that was in your mom's room," Shelley began, "and she told me to tell you it's now in *your* room. It's something of a religious nature . . . I think it might have a *Mary* connotation . . . and she also wants you to know that there's going to be some sort of mix-up with the flowers, the pink carnations . . . in the next few days. And also, she's showing me hand-carved Jesus faces made of wood, and I think they're from Italy . . . she likes them. . . . "

I was listening, but in my head I had another whole mental commentary going on that was worthy of the most stubborn cynic. As I sat in bed, I scanned my room from floor to ceiling. Nope, there was *nothing* of a "religious nature" in here, I told her. Shelley was just plain wrong. Then this whole mix-up with the flowers . . . how would I know if there was going to be a mix-up at the wake? I'd have to wait. And the hand-carved, wooden, Italian Jesus references? I just laughed at that one. I used to tease Shelley, who was Jewish, that she had "Catholic envy." She didn't, of course, but she was fascinated with the religion. I told her to lay off the Catholic references because she was *all wrong.* I could tell by her voice that she was getting a bit indignant at my reaction. I'm sure she was thinking that I wasn't appreciating her time and energy, especially since she had hernia surgery pending the next day.

Two days later, we all dressed up and went to my cousin's wedding. An hour before the ceremony, there was indeed a mix-up with the flowers for the wedding party. The flower shop was supposed to send white carnations for us to wear, but instead sent pink—which clashed with the bouquet. That was validation hit number one.

The next day was the first day of the wake. What I remember most vividly was the vision of Shelley hobbling into the funeral home that day. I say "hobble," because she had just had her surgery, and upon being discharged from the hospital, she forced her husband to take her to the funeral home instead of going straight home like the doctor ordered. It wasn't so much to pay respects to my mother because, as far as Shelley was concerned, the two ladies had already had their private "visit" with each other the morning Mom crossed. Instead, it was to check in on me and make sure I was hanging in there.

After my mother passed, Shelley insisted that I call her every night and "download" the events of the day because she wanted to make sure I didn't bottle up my emotions. She wanted me to know I had a friend who was ready to talk and who was just a phone call away.

As everyone gathered together at the wake, I noticed a string of rosary beads hanging on the inside of the casket and leaned in to take a closer look. They were hand-carved, Italian-made, wooden rosary beads, each bead shaped in the face of Jesus. I immediately investigated where they'd come from and found out that they'd been sent by my mother's older sister, Rachel, who'd picked them out on a whim. Validation hit number two.

Later that night when I returned home, I walked into my bedroom, turned the light on, and gasped at what I saw.

The day Shelley had called me with my mom's messages, I'd been sitting up in bed leaning up against my headboard as we talked on the phone. But it wasn't really a headboard . . . it was the mirror from the bureau in my mother's room that used to be positioned directly opposite her bed. Due to her deteriorating condition, the family had thought it best to take the mirror down so she didn't have to stare at herself all the time and constantly be reminded of how sick she was. The only other place the mirror would fit was right behind my headboard, and oh, yeah, taped up to the mirror was a picture of the Sacred Heart of Jesus and a photo that was taken at an apparition site of the Blessed Mother in Medjugoria, Yugoslavia.

I couldn't see any of these things when I was talking to Shelley on the phone because they were behind my head as we spoke. Standing in the doorway of my bedroom, I looked at those photos and wept uncontrollably. I called Shelley at around 2 A.M. and told her about all the validations that day and apologized to her for not being appreciative of her time and friendship that morning on the phone. She told me it was all right, not to worry—that's what friends were for.

ENGAGEMENT DAY

SHELLEY PROVED TO BE A CONDUIT between my mother and me again and again, passing along her messages. It was like she was my mom's personal secretary here on this side. Why didn't my mother just come directly to me, you ask? That would seem the simpler way, but really it isn't. Before she passed, I distinctly instructed my mother that when she wanted to connect with me from the Other Side, to go through someone like Shelley. I knew that if I got things psychically from my mom, I wouldn't trust the information because I was too close to her. I would worry that what I was getting would be jumbled up with my emotions and memories, and brought on because I missed her.

When it comes to anyone close to me coming through from the Other Side, I trust the process better if the information is coming via another psychic, especially Shelley, who always let me know that Mom was around me during the most intimate, joyous occasions of my life.

IT WAS THE FALL OF 1993, and I'd just picked up Sandra's engagement ring—a pear-shaped diamond with three small chips on each side. I'd bought it from friends of friends who worked in Manhattan's diamond district.

I was very excited about popping the question a few weeks later, but first I had to make sure that Mom knew of my purchase. I got into my car, opened up the ring box, and held it up: "Mom, you're the first one to see the ring!" I said out loud. I drove home with a smile on my face, and when I got there, I had two blinking messages on my answering machine.

"John . . . it's Shelley. If you're there, pick up. Your mother won't let me get any work done today. Call me back as soon as you get this message." *Click.*

"John . . . it's me again . . . all right, I know this can't be true, and what your mom is telling me must be far off, because I know we're such good friends that you would have told me about this . . . but she's so damn excited . . . call me back!" *Click.*

In the back of my mind, I was hoping that Shelley had gotten a message about the ring from my mother, but I didn't want to think about it and get my hopes up. I dialed Shelley's number, and when she answered, she told me that my mother had been "hanging out" with her all morning and was very excited to tell her I was getting married. Shelley was perplexed by this message, because even though she'd accurately (and eerily) predicted that I'd end up with Sandra in a reading she'd done about seven years earlier, I hadn't told her yet about my potential engagement.

"Your mother is all excited, and she said you showed her the ring 'first'? Does this make sense to you? What's she talking about? Am I cracking up or what?"

Please imagine that you're me and you're sitting on the edge of the bed, listening to Shelley deliver this message—confused but with spot-on precision—all the while staring at the ring in your hand. This was just another moment of my being wowed and amazed by her uncanny accuracy.

I confessed to her that it was true . . . and we went out and celebrated over a hamburger deluxe and a roast pork sandwich with extra duck sauce (of course).

Shelley was to astound me with her accuracy again and again during our friendship. Shortly after I moved to Huntington, Long Island, Sandra asked me to do a small group reading for her mother and a few of her mom's friends. I called Shelley and invited her over for dinner. What she didn't know was that she was going to work for her supper that night as well. I sprang it on her at the last minute when I picked her up at her house, telling her I had this group to do . . . would she mind participating? She laughed and said she already knew she was going to be working that night—her guides had told her, and she'd meditated in preparation before I picked her up (yes . . . she was *that* good).

We started the group, and some amazing details started to come through about my mother-in-law's family. The funny part of it, though, was that Sandra had to act as "guest medium" during the group because the women we were reading only spoke Portuguese. Shelley and I joked that we would say a sentence, and Sandra would translate what seemed like four paragraphs. We were convinced that Sandra was adding in a bit of her own "translation" of the Other Side as well. But it was during this group that Shelley rendered me speechless for the second time in the almost 15 years that I'd known her.

The first time was when my Uncle Carmine had died. I'd asked her to do a reading for my cousin, his daughter, Little Ro, and she agreed. A few hours before the session, Little Ro and I were having a bite to eat at a local diner, and I saw Shelley across the room in another booth. (Yes, both of us practically *lived* at diners.) I went over to her table to say hello and to tell her I really, really appreciated that she was squeezing my cousin in for a session instead of putting her on her long waiting list. And then I made the gravest error possible.

"I just hope," I continued, "that her dad . . . my Uncle Carmine . . . comes through for her and . . . "

"Damn it, John!" I thought she was going to hit me. "I can't believe you just told me her father died and that's who she wants to connect with . . . *and you told me his name!"* What was I thinking? One of the first things you learn in Basic Mediumship 101 is to never divulge anything ahead of time so the integrity of the experience won't be violated. That doesn't mean you should be cagey and evasive. Quite the contrary, you should validate what does or doesn't make sense . . . but don't offer information, which is what I'd just done. Shelley immediately wanted to cancel the session.

I stood up and firmly told her that if I had to march back to my table and tell my cousin I just messed up her chance to talk to her dad—whom she missed and loved so desperately—because of a stupid mistake on my part . . . well, I just couldn't do it. Shelley begrudgingly agreed to go on with the session, but she was clearly annoyed with me.

About an hour and a half later, we arrived on Shelley's doorstep. She welcomed my cousin and me into her beautiful home and directed us to sit in the breakfast nook off her kitchen. Little Ro sat there waiting, nervous—but I assure you, not more nervous than I. For the entire car ride over, I was praying to her father to come through, despite my pre-reading faux pas.

When it was time, Shelley invited my cousin into the den for the reading. Ro asked Shelley if I could sit in on the session, and Shelley said that was fine, even though she was still a bit ticked off at for me for making her job more difficult than it needed to be. Now, both she and Uncle Carmine were going to have to work twice as hard since I'd already given away some prime validating information.

The reading lasted over an hour, and Shelley came through with dozens upon dozens of accurate details about my uncle—from the clothes he wore to the location where he lived—it was like she was reading from a list compiled by Uncle Carmine himself. She even "embodied" him at one point during the session by mimicking what he'd do and say, capturing his gestures. My cousin laughed and cried, and I took notes so she wouldn't forget a word. Then, near the end of the reading, Shelley looked over at me, her face beaming.

With a burst of confidence, she declared: "Why . . . his name isn't Carmine . . . it's *Carmen!*"

Oops, strike one for Shelley, I thought. I put a big "X" down on the piece of paper where I was keeping a tally of validations. Or, wait . . . maybe there was another energy on the Other Side Shelley was going to bring through who also had a "C" name. I was racking my brain trying to think of another "C" name, when I heard my cousin reply, "Yes!"

"What?!" I asked, totally interrupting the session (another no-no).

"His real name is Carmen, not Carmine," Ro explained.

"But . . . Carmen is a woman's name!"

Little Ro explained that it was the Italian way to spell it like that, and that Carmen really *was* his official name, I just didn't know it. My big error at the diner gave Uncle Carmine an opportunity to come through with an even more detailed and obscure validation about himself that only intimate family members knew. Hurray for him. That night, I saw a change in my cousin, as if a weight had been lifted. She knew that her daddy was still with her.

The group session in my living room with Sandra's relatives was about to be an instant replay of that kind of *Wow!* validation. Shelley and I were delivering messages as a team, alternating like a relay duo passing the baton as we brought them through. Then, as I was finishing one message, I felt Shelley staring at me. She was sitting in a chair to my left and had turned to fully face me with this inquisitive look on her face.

"You wore your mother's nameplate under your tuxedo on your wedding day?"

Pow!

My jaw hit the floor. The day I got married, as I was getting dressed, I looked at my mother's picture and told her out loud that I was going to keep her with me that day by wearing her nameplate that said "Princess" under my tuxedo shirt. Nobody, not even Sandra, knew I did this, and quite honestly, up until that moment when Shelley made that statement, I'd almost forgotten about it. But at that second, the emotions I felt so long ago came back to me, and I couldn't speak. My eyes welled up, I looked down, then I looked over to Sandra and smiled—then back to Shelley.

"I did . . . I did wear that nameplate!" I told her. "Thank you for that."

THE GREETING COMMITTEE

OVER THE YEARS, I watched as Shelley developed an uncanny ability to connect with extremely recent passings during her readings, whether it was during a private session or a group reading. Neither of us could figure out exactly how she was able to do this, but I think it was just part of who she was and what her job was here in this world. One evening in 1994 when she and I were giving a talk at a seminar called "Gifts of Love" at the Smithtown Sheraton in Long Island, she made a connection with a man who'd lost his wife a few days before. Everybody in the audience was shocked and very moved—not the least being Shelley herself, who at one point (in her trademark, blunt, mother-from-Queens fashion) asked the man, "What are you *doing* here? So recently after your wife's passing? You should be at home!"

Another night when Shelley accompanied me on one of my group readings in New Jersey, she also brought through a woman's son who had crossed a few days earlier. Then there was a benefit I organized for Hospice Care of Long Island where I asked Shelley and Lydia Clar (the woman who'd given me my first reading) to read the audience. We all did good work that evening, but I must say, Shelley's messages were so detailed and specific that on more than one occasion she brought the entire room to tears. I was standing in the back of the room, listening, admiring, and watching my friend do her thing when she connected with the spirit of a grandmother of one person, and then another woman's son, both of whom had passed within the month.

"John . . . where are you? Are you still in the room?"

"I'm back here, Shelley. . . ."

"Here I go again . . . what is it that you call me?"

"The Greeting Committee!"

Shelley told the entire room how I tease her with that nickname at these events because you could put her in a room full of people and she'd connect with the most recent passing. I decided that one of her purposes in having this ability was to be the first one to say *hello* to people who were new to the Other Side. I kept threatening to get her a sweatshirt that said "Greeting Committee" on it. She made me promise in front of everyone at that benefit that I *would* finally buy her that shirt after all these years. I wish I had.

In June of 2001, the friend and teacher I had known for half my life made her transition to the Other Side after succumbing to cancer. In a way, it was like a déjà vu of losing my mother. I'd been keeping tabs on Shelley's condition throughout her illness, since we always spoke with each other two to three times a day at length.

Then I noticed that our calls were becoming shorter and less frequent, usually ending with Shelley asking if she could call me back later because she was feeling tired. When she asked me if I thought her diagnosis was terminal, I could not—would not—answer. I knew it was because I was shown this by my guides. But even when her family pressed me to answer that question, I was evasive in my response—perhaps because I held out hope and faith that she could beat this, despite what my guides told me. I didn't want to it to be true.

Shelley split her time between her apartment in Bayside, Queens, and her house in Vermont. (Her husband, Marvin, had passed about ten years before.) Shelley's daughter would graciously call me and give me updates about what was happening and what the doctors were saying.

One afternoon I got a message on my answering machine from her daughter with the usual update, but this time I stopped in my tracks when I heard it. There wasn't anything emotional or urgent about this particular message, but there was something about her daughter's tone that made me feel I needed to see Shelley right away and that this visit would be our last.

I called the *Crossing Over* producers and cancelled two tapings I was to do that day, and within minutes, Carol had printed up driving directions to the hospital in Vermont off the Internet. An hour later, I was heading north on the freeway without a suitcase or a change of clothes or even a toothbrush . . . and without telling my wife. I called Sandra from the car and told her I was somewhere in New England and I wouldn't be home for dinner.

She completely understood—Sandra and Shelley had struck up a great connection of their own, and we'd spent many a Jewish holiday together, with Sandra always teasing Shelley that one of these days she was going to have to feed her a big bowl of matzoh ball soup like a proper Jewish mother should. That was their little joke together.

The entire drive to the hospital, I listened to an Enya CD. I've always loved her voice and music, but when she released the song "Only Time," it immediately reminded me of Shelley. And here I was, months later, driving up to see my friend for the last time . . . realizing that the song is correct. In life, we have only time. But how long, we never know.

According to my Internet directions, my drive to the hospital should have taken me about four hours. But when I got to the hospital, after getting lost (please, no psychic jokes about that), it was seven hours later. Still, I was able to spend a couple of hours with Shelley alone, even though she slept through most of my stay. When she did wake up, I think she was a bit alarmed to see me. Not that she thought she had crossed over or anything . . . but seeing me would have tipped her off that the time was near.

I put her mind at ease and even got her to smile a few times. At this stage in her illness, Shelley had lost mobility and wasn't able to speak. At one point, she was trying to tell me something, and she was mouthing it, but I couldn't understand her. I didn't realize it, but one of the nurses had walked into the room and was standing behind me when I said, "Shell, look at me. Whatever you're trying to say . . . *send* it to me. . . . " Meaning, telepathically send me the message and see if I can get it. Immediately, my head began to itch . . . and I asked her if she wanted me to scratch her head. She nodded and I scratched, much to her relief.

"Wow! How cool was that?" the nurse standing behind me piped up. "What is that, some psychic thing? I heard that Mrs. Peck is a psychic. Is that really true?"

I smiled, looked at the nurse, and then back at Shelley, and said, "Not only is Shelley Peck one of the country's top psychic mediums, but she's also a great astrologer and numerologist. But to me, she's my buddy." I winked, and Shelley smiled. I stood there for a couple of hours watching her, going over our relationship and my memories in a weird, fast-forward kind of way. I waited for her to fall asleep before I left after midnight, way past official visiting hours.

Shelley crossed over just a few days later.

I WANT YOU TO KNOW that while writing this chapter, I had to stop a number of times because the memories opened up my emotional floodgates. I could barely type through my smiles and tears. I always say that our tears are a tribute to the feelings we have for our loved ones, so we should never hold them back. It's not a sign of weakness or sadness, but instead, a physical sign of our appreciation and affection for them.

People ask me all the time if I've heard from Shelley since she passed. Because of the connection I had with her, she falls into the same category as my own family. She was so close to me that I can't be objective about whether she's coming through to me or if I'm just thinking about her. But there was a connection one night three months after she passed that I'm certain of.

I had just come back from a group reading in New Jersey, and I was to meet Sandra at the home of our good friends, Jon and Stacy. The whole car ride there, I couldn't get Shelley out of my mind, and I knew it was her way of letting me know that she was around. Our teachers, our friends, and our spirit guides on the Other Side are always around us, sending signals that they're taking care of us and guiding us on our path. And the guidance and love we get from our teachers and friends on this earth doesn't stop once they cross over, but continues on a higher plane.

On the way to meet Sandra, I decided to stop by my office in Huntington to use the rest room because the drive was a bit longer than I had anticipated. When I walked into my empty office, there was a video on my desk marked "Shelley"—it was a taped interview she'd given the year before for a cable-TV special called *Messages from the Dead*, which launched my show, *Crossing Over*. The producers of that show had heard that Shelley had crossed over and had sent me her entire, unedited interview to keep.

I slipped the tape into the VCR and sat on my couch in the office, watching and hearing my old friend laugh and speak about our relationship. There were moments on that tape I'd never seen before.

"What makes John special?" the interviewer asked her. My ears perked up at this one.

"What *doesn't* make John special is a better question," she answered. "He's the type of person who would drop everything he's doing and run to wherever you are if you needed him. I know he would do that for me if I ever needed him. "

To me, it was as if she'd made a psychic prediction during that interview and was now showing it to me from beyond the grave. In that interview, she basically recounted my rush to the hospital a few days before she left this world. And as I listened to her, I couldn't help but cry. Even though I'm a medium and I know she's all right and still around . . . I miss her.

CHAPTER EIGHT

The 9/11 Factor

I BELIEVE THAT WE ALL DECIDE when to leave our physical body and "go home" or "join God." I don't think most of us are aware of this choice on a conscious level, although some people who are highly attuned to the spiritual world, including children, sometimes are. But mostly, it's a subconscious "knowing" of the soul that it's time to leave this realm and move onward to the next one. Perhaps we've learned all we're capable of learning or need to learn here, and understand it's our time to "graduate." Or perhaps our leaving also involves teaching other people left behind important lessons of their own that they'll learn as a result of our departure.

But although I believe we choose *when,* I'm not necessarily sure if we choose *how*—that is, I don't know if we can decide upon our method of departure. If we could, I'd guess that most people would pass on in a loving and pain-free manner . . . maybe drifting off to sleep in a loved one's arms. Then there would be the adventurous types who'd want to do it while jumping out of a plane or scaling Mt. Everest.

But the reality of life is that death is rarely peaceful, pretty, or fun for that matter. Even with my strong belief that we choose when we cross over, like anyone else I still have trouble coming to terms with the fact that so many people die violent or cruel deaths—which brings up this question for many: If there *is* a God, how could He or She make us suffer unduly? And what about tragedies we endure, such as earthquakes or volcanoes or plane crashes that kill hundreds at a time?

The most recent tragedy still on all of our minds, which has become part of the fabric of our lives in New York City, is the terrorist attack on the World Trade Center on September 11, 2001. In a few horrible moments, thousands of innocent lives were taken, and scores of families were left heartbroken and stunned, wondering why. It's difficult for me to answer that question except to say that, in keeping with what I believe and as hard it is to hear, all the people who crossed over in the attack that day needed to go on to the next spiritual level at the same time. In fact, since the attack, I've probably conducted hundreds of readings that are September 11-related, and many energies have come through saying as such— that it was their "time," and they had to move on to other work at the next level.

After September 11, I received countless letters, e-mails, and phone calls from people who had lost loved ones that day, anxious to get a reading. Normally I'm a stickler about anyone skipping ahead on the long waiting list I have for personal sessions, but in this case, I felt I had to make an exception. First, I needed to feel that I was doing my part, like everyone else, to help the country heal after the disaster. Second, I figured that giving out socks or canned goods at Ground Zero wouldn't be using my abilities to their best advantage. I needed to do what *I* do—make connections for these people who were in pain and let them know that their loved ones were safe and well on the Other Side. My staff and I randomly chose families to come in for sessions, and I saw them on my personal time on evenings and weekends. I insisted that these families speak to grief counselors both before and after a reading since it was still so soon after the tragedy.

As I've said earlier, I don't usually remember the readings I do after they're over. By the next day, any details are wiped from my memory forever. But there have been a handful of sessions, especially in the last two years, that have left an indelible impression on me. During one seminar in Long Island, about six weeks after the World Trade Center attack, I was doing a reading on one side of the room when I was suddenly seized by a new energy coming through. It was a firefighter calling out the name of his wife, Nancy. I felt a forceful pull toward a pretty woman sitting in the second row.

Nancy Carroll had come to the seminar from Ridgewood, New Jersey, in the hopes of connecting with her husband, Michael, a firefighter who had died on 9/11. She was given a ticket to the seminar by a friend who had bought it in July—two months before the attack. Not only did Michael come through that day with details of Nancy's life since he'd passed (and details of events still to happen), but he also came through with his signature sense of humor.

John: I have a rescue worker coming through [looking at one woman, then pointing directly at her]. Are you Nancy?

Nancy: Yes, I am.

John: I have a Michael coming through. Do you understand this? He passed on September 11th.

Nancy: Yes . . . yes, I do.

John: I don't know if he's a fireman or a cop, but here we go. He's showing me a gavel, but I have no idea what it means.

Nancy: I do. His friend was killed with him . . . his name was Michael Judge. He was a chaplain for the fire department.

John: Wow. Okay—and he wants to acknowledge Robert.

Nancy: That's his friend, a firefighter, who gave his eulogy at his memorial.

John: And he's telling me there's another Nancy he wants to acknowledge. Not you . . . a different Nancy.

Nancy: Yes . . . his sister.

John: Connected with her . . . there's a changing of companies or something.

Nancy: Yes! Nancy and I have been running Michael's small business since he died . . . and we're selling the business this week.

John: He also says a very special hello to Billy.

Nancy: That's his brother . . . he's a retired fire captain.

John: He says Billy isn't doing well, and the family needs to know that . . .

Nancy: Yes, I think that's true. He's very upset about Michael.

John: He says he's glad you "turned down the reporter," whatever that means. He says the reporter didn't have the children's best interests at heart. That they were only interested in the story. Do you know what this means?

Nancy: Yes, I do! A news show called me and wanted to do a story on my kids . . . but I didn't feel right about it and I said no . . .

John: Okay. Now, do you have a picture of Michael that was in the newspaper? He's says it's a picture of him rescuing a girl.

Nancy: Yes! I was just looking at this!

John: Because Michael says he was with you when you were looking at this picture. He also says they'll give you what you want that's connected with you. You will get it . . . whatever this means. . . .

Nancy: Okay . . .

John: He says the Florida trip is postponed, not cancelled.

Nancy: We were supposed to go to Florida a month after he was killed.

John: Did your daughter have a dream recently that was very shocking to you?

Nancy: Yes!

John: Michael was with her in that dream, he wants you to know that. And he says he enjoyed his memorial. He says that Mayor Giuliani was there.

Nancy: Yes, he was!

John: And he's telling me that right now . . . there are people at the site who are being injured in some way.

Nancy: I'm not sure what you mean.

John: I don't know either, but he's saying people at the site are injured, and there's a "DN" connection to you involving that. Okay . . . [pause, then sarcastically], he says, "Now aren't you glad I didn't wear my ring to work?"

Nancy: Yes! Because I get to have his ring now!

John: Michael tells me he's a Catholic and you pray for him. He thanks you for his prayers. He says they help him tremendously. He tells me you carry his rosary beads with you.

Nancy: I do!

John (laughing): Oh . . . hold on. He also tells me you carry a 5-by-7 picture of him!

Nancy: Well, I don't usually . . . but it's in my purse now!

John: And [laughing] he tells me he's such a good-looking guy!

Nancy: Yes! He looks like JFK, Jr.

John: It's very important for his family to know that he's still doing what he did here. He's still a rescue worker on the Other Side. And Michael tells me there's something important happening this weekend in the town you live in.

Nancy: Yes, 12 people in our town were killed on 9/11. We're having a special ceremony for all of them. I'm going to that.

John: He wants you to look out for a bird on that day. He says it's a validation that he's always with you. There's going to be some kind of a sign with a bird.

Nancy: Okay.

One week later, on the morning of the ceremony, Nancy was awakened by loud noises in the house and her mother shaking her by the shoulders. "She said, 'Nancy, wake up . . . there's a giant bird flapping around in the bathroom!'" The two women raced down the hall to find that a stray bird had somehow gotten through a crack in the open window and was now trapped in the bathroom, flailing about, with no intention of leaving. Nancy was shocked. Could the "sign" have been more obvious? She didn't think so. After trying to usher the bird out the window themselves, Nancy and her mother called Animal Control to come and get it.

"I told my mom, 'Well . . . I guess this is my bird!'" But even without such a dramatic signal, Nancy had no doubt that her husband had come through "like gangbusters" in the reading the week before, and he'd be with her on this day and always.

By the time Nancy had come to the seminar, the hope she'd held on to for days—that her husband had survived the World Trade Center collapse—was gone. Together since they were teenagers and married for 13 years, she described their relationship as soul mates who "couldn't wait for the other to walk through the door at the end of the day." As Nancy explained some of the details her husband came through with during the reading, the rest of the seminar attendees gasped.

"The photo of my husband in the newspaper was a picture of him coming out of a building, holding his hat over a woman's head to protect her. I had framed it and put it up in the living room. And Michael said to me at the time, 'Why would you frame this one? It's not like it's a rescue or anything! It's ridiculous!' But I really liked the photo. The night before I came to the seminar, I was looking at the picture, and I was feeling really annoyed at him . . . annoyed that he had 'left' me. And I flung the picture across the room and said out loud, *'How could you leave me?!'*" But as Nancy found out, he hadn't really left her. In fact, he was with her at that moment when she'd been in such pain. Similarly, he'd been at home to comfort their three-year-old daughter, Olivia, through the pain of missing her daddy. In a vivid dream just three weeks after September 11, Olivia had a "play date" with her dad who was on the Other Side.

"My daughter had been very sad, and she really missed her father playing with her," recalled Nancy. "Michael had just put up one of those wooden play gyms in the yard, and he loved to play with Olivia on it. She was so sad. But one morning she came downstairs and was so happy. She told me, 'I had a dream that Daddy came into my room, got me dressed, took me out to my new play gym to play, and then took me to McDonald's!' She was in a great mood." Nancy didn't know it at the time, but her daughter had experienced a "visit" from her daddy, which he confirmed in the reading.

Not only did Michael come through with specifics that only Nancy knew about, but she was struck by the *way* he had come through with them—for example, his joking about her having his wedding ring. "Michael had been a fireman for 16 years, and when he went to the academy, they were taught to never wear jewelry on the job," said Nancy. "He'd come home from work and say, 'Darn, I left my ring and watch in my locker!' Then he wouldn't be due in to work for another two days, and it would drive him crazy because he didn't have his ring or watch on. I used to always tell him, 'Why don't you just wear them while you work?' but he wouldn't do it. Three days after September 11th, when I realized that he probably wasn't coming home, I went to his locker to get his backpack. And there were his wedding ring and his watch sitting there. I was so happy to have these things—I was so happy he'd left them there. I put his wedding ring around a long chain, and I wear it around my neck." Nancy pulled the ring out from under her sweater and showed the group.

There were a few details in the reading that didn't make sense to Nancy at the time, but which were validated in the weeks to come. She couldn't figure out what Michael meant when he said people were being hurt down at Ground Zero, so she called up Michael's station the next day to check on it.

"I called up and asked the guy who answered, 'What happened down there last night?' and he said, 'Oh, the cops were telling us we couldn't dig.'" As it turns out, the night of the seminar was a very tense, violent night down at Ground Zero. The firemen had been digging nonstop to find people in the rubble, including their comrades, and wanted to continue, "but the police were harassing them and roughhousing them," the firefighter on the phone said.

After Nancy hung up, she realized that the name of the fire-fighter she'd just been speaking to was connected to the message. This firefighter, who was a buddy of Michael's, was in the famous photo that appeared in the media all over the world—the picture of three firefighters hoisting a flag up at the disaster site. His name is Danny—the "DN" connected to the message in the reading. The final mystery, when Michael said that Nancy would receive what was "connected" to her, was solved a few weeks later. Michael's body was recovered from the disaster site and returned home for a hero's burial.

"When I went home after the reading," Nancy remembered, "I felt such peace. Michael and I had so much together, and something like that just doesn't go away. Even now, I still feel very connected to him. Since the reading, I talk to him constantly. I don't know why September 11th happened . . . I guess I'll know when I get to the Other Side myself. Maybe I have my own life lessons to learn. And sometimes I wonder . . . if 2,000 people were going to die at once, maybe God needed 400 good firefighters up there to help them all with the transition. Firefighters are such good people, such help-ful souls, who only want to help others. That's the kind of man my husband was—and *is*. I know he's out there and listening to me, and I know this because of the reading."

Michael Carroll was one of the first firefighters to come through to me so soon after September 11, and it was a very emotional night for me, for Nancy, and for everybody in the room. I still remem-ber how brave and proud Nancy was as she sat up straight in the chair, taking in the information and validating it with such pride and love for her hero husband.

When the seminar was over, Nancy approached me up front and gave me her husband's mass card—which had his picture on it for remembrance.

Then, as further validation to me that Michael was still around, two days later I was given another token of this firefighter's brav-ery. At another, separate seminar, a young man approached me who had heard about the September 11-related readings I'd been doing and wanted to say a general thank you from all the families I was helping. As a gift, he handed me a T-shirt that was made in honor of the firefighters. At that time, the firehouses were making up shirts with individual names of their brothers and sisters they'd lost on the back. This man handed me a navy blue T-shirt with a firefighter emblem on it, and as he did, I felt a twinge of familiarity.

As soon as I got home, I raced to my desk to check the name on the Mass card Nancy had given me with the name on the shirt. Sure enough, it was the same name. On the back of the T-shirt were the words in bold: *In Loving Memory of Michael T Caroll* [sic]. It was yet another hello from Michael, who was now rescuing and helping others on the Other Side on a grand scale.

To this day, I keep that Mass card and the T-shirt at home—the card is on my work desk, and the shirt is carefully folded in my "special" drawer of items that have great meaning to me. Each time I sit at my desk, I see the card, and I think of Michael and Nancy and their ongoing love that transcends the boundaries of the human body.

My link with Nancy and the Other Side continues. Last May, Nancy was roaming through a bookstore and saw the new paperback version of *CROSSING OVER: The Stories Behind the Stories*, on the bookshelf with the added 9/11 chapter. "I bought it and took it home and leafed through it, wondering if my reading was mentioned," Nancy said. She fell asleep a bit disappointed, with the book on her lap, open to the 9/11 chapter. Her reading wasn't in there. The very next day, she got a telephone call from Natasha—who'd been trying to track her down for weeks—asking if she'd be a part of this book, *After Life*. "I couldn't believe it!" Nancy exclaimed.

Looking back, the link between Nancy and the man who gave me the T-shirt may have surprised me then, but doesn't now. In the two years since the terrorist attacks, I've witnessed a sort of spiritual phenomenon I've never seen before—a banding together of families linked to 9/11 on the Other Side. During my group readings in the New York-New Jersey area and my many tapings of *Crossing Over,* anytime there's someone in the room who suffered a loss due to 9/11, their loved one who comes through for them will then bring through other 9/11 losses. Even if these people who died didn't know each other at all in life, their mutual bond in how they passed is so intense that they act as "family" and link up to help each other.

I've done a number of seminars and groups where for the first two hours only 9/11 energies have come through. It kind of feels like they take me hostage and won't let me go. Once one of them gets my attention, they form a chain of sorts and bring in the rest of their 9/11 "family" to dominate the group. Now bear in mind, this phenomenon doesn't happen all the time. So if you're sitting in a seminar where all these 9/11 families are showing up left and right and your loved one who also passed in 9/11 doesn't come through, please don't be upset. Although I see it happen often, the 9/11 factor isn't a given at every event. It doesn't mean your loved one isn't okay or doesn't want to talk to you. It just means I cannot, as always, get to every person and each energy that wants to make a connection.

After many months of experiencing this banding together of souls, I had to admire their tenacity. And because this exclusive "family" pushes everyone else's family aside and holds me hostage, I began calling them a nickname—"The 9/11 Factor." And if anyone out there is offended by this nickname, please know that I use the phrase with humor, and with that humor is respect and a bit of awe. And make no mistake—that's how the other energies on the Other Side feel about The 9/11 factor, too. Because as they strong-arm their way and cut to the front of the line, the families on the Other Side who are *not* 9/11-related dutifully bow their heads and stand aside.

LAST DECEMBER 2002, I conducted several group readings in New York overrun by this 9/11 tag team. I didn't know it at the time, but in one group in Secaucus, New Jersey, Nancy Carroll had returned and was sitting in the back. With her, she had brought along some extended members of the her new 9/11 family—other women who had also lost their husbands at the World Trade Center. These five women had been strangers to one another one year earlier. They met in a 9/11 support group in New Jersey and had since become friends.

Nancy had told the group about her first reading when Michael came through with flying colors, but the women were very skeptical, to say the least. Here's an example of how the 9/11 family on the Other Side passes the baton from member to member. In this case, it was a situation involving five husbands, all on the same team, trying to get hold of the ball and shoot. They were coming through to me so fast that I could barely keep up and match the husbands to the corresponding wives. The wives, too, were getting confused.

John: I have an older female who passes from cancer. Helen, Ellen, Eileen. And there's a March connection. Someone's coming through claiming to be a mother figure, and there's a connection to March.

Woman #1: I have a birthday in March . . . my husband has an Aunt Helen.

John: Your husband has passed, right?

Woman #1: Yes.

John: Did you lose someone on 9/11?

Woman #1: Yes.

John: Helen is telling me . . . wait . . . .

I then felt the pull move to two other women sitting nearby. It switched gears and pointed to them . . .

John: Wait . . . you two also lost someone on 9/11?

Woman #2 and Woman#3 (together): Yes.

John: Where's the Michael?

Woman #2: My son.

Woman #3: . . . and my husband.

John: There is an "A" connection. And someone's birthday is coming up in January.

Woman #2: Yes.

John (pointing to Woman #3): You have two kids?

Woman #3: Yes.

John: Who has the ongoing heart problem?

Woman #2: My dad.

John: Your husband is saying he has to watch it . . .

I felt a new energy try to get my attention. To a fourth woman sitting with them, I posed a question.

John: Did you lose a husband on 9/11, too?

Woman #4: Yes.

John: I'm bringing through someone connected to the number six.

Woman #4: My son is connected to a six.

John: Does someone have a Steve?

Woman #4: I'm connected to a Steve.

John: Is he a smartass? If he was here, would he be making jokes about all of this?

Woman #4: Oh, yeah.

John: I have to acknowledge that someone wrote his name in cement.

Woman #4: Yes, we did.

John: I also have to acknowledge you have his chain.

Woman #4: Yes . . . I do.

John: Does he have a major connection to the name Britney? I'm seeing Britney Spears. Or does he have a huge affinity with Britney Spears.

Woman #4: My daughter loves Britney. She's going to the Jingle Ball tomorrow night.

John: I wouldn't be surprised if Britney shows up there.

Again, I felt a new energy joining the team on the Other Side and was pulled to yet another woman in the group here on this side.

John: Where's the Chris [pointing to Woman #5]? Are you connected to the Chris?

Woman #5: My husband is Chris.

John: He's making me feel like I need to talk about your clothes. Did you just go on a spending spree? Did you change sizes? He's making me feel like your skirt doesn't fit you anymore.

Woman #5: I'm three sizes smaller now.

John: He says two days before September 11th, you had a very special day.

Woman #5: Yes, it was our anniversary.

John: He says he'll never forget it.

Once again, I felt another new energy arrive on the scene. . . .

John: Where's John?

Woman #6: My husband is John.

John: He's apologizing for the mortgage. What does that mean?

Woman #6: We moved just two months before he passed.

John: Is he the one who would pick you up and throw you over his shoulder?

Woman #6: Every night, he did that with my little one.

John: Do all these guys know each other?

All the women in unison: No.

John: Were you all taking bets before you got here as to which husband would come through tonight?

All women in unison: Yes . . . we were!

The reading continued in this way, bouncing around from wife to wife, with each woman getting a snippet of information before a new husband butted in. At one point, it felt like that scene in the movie *Ghost,* when Whoopi Goldberg was surrounded by a crowd of spirits all trying to talk to their relatives at the same time. If I didn't know better, I would have guessed that all these husbands coming through were brothers because of the kinship feeling I was getting attached to them, and because they kept bringing through each new energy like they were introducing a new family member into the equation. But while the husbands were working hard to get through to their wives, not all of the women were appreciative of their efforts. At one point, one wife who had gotten a few details during the reading put up her hand.

"When are you going to say something specific?" she demanded. "When are you going to say something that will make me, or any of us, know this is for real? I mean . . . do you all believe this?"

There was a hush in the room. At that moment, part of me wanted to grab this woman by the collar and slap her silly. I was working my ass off trying to reunite her with her family, and I knew that the energies were working their asses off, too. And through it all, she sits there wearing "The Face" (what I call the arms crossed/mouth-pinched look that skeptics sometimes give me), making me feel that she was insulting the process.

I must admit that I'm intolerant of this type of behavior. I don't believe that the loss of a loved one gives someone the right to be mean or to make demands, especially of someone who's trying to help. If you ever find yourself in a situation where you're lashing out at people because you're suffering a loss, take a moment to think about what you're doing. Maybe the people you're lashing out at are those closest to you, and those who are trying to help you deal with the tragedy or loss.

Initially, I reacted to her question out of ego. *"I know you must be kidding!* I thought that's what I *was* doing."

She just shook her head and folded her arms as the rest of the room stared at her in disbelief. I'm not going to identify which woman this was, but I will say that she had several validations throughout the reading that were accurate and specific.

Nancy Carroll, who had come with the woman, acknowledged these validations: "She was getting some good information that I knew was right, but she still wasn't buying it," Nancy said. "Then I realized that maybe these women didn't have the background I had. I had read your books and watched *Crossing Over,* and I knew how it all worked, so when the information started flying at me like that, I could decipher it. These women walked in with certain expectations. They were like, 'I want John to come through with my nickname,' but it doesn't work that way." During a break in the seminar, Nancy came up to me and apologized for her friend's behavior.

"You've got to tell your friends that they can't be like this when the energies come across," I said. "Because if they are, the energies will never come through again." And it's true. If these energies are not "welcomed" or think we're taking their attempts to make contact as a joke, they won't bother to come back. Why should they? Would you visit a friend or relative who slammed a door in your face?

This is why I always, always warn people at the beginning of a session that they can't enter into this process with fixed expectations or wearing blinders. I can't stress this point enough. If you approach a session with a closed mind, you'll miss the messages and be disappointed no matter what happens.

After this woman gave me "The Face" and "The Tone," I took a deep breath and counted to five, trying to suppress my rising anger. I reminded myself that this woman was still wrestling with her loss and had a long way to go before she came to terms with it. To her, by validating what was going on in the room that day, she'd have to acknowledge the death of her husband—something she didn't want to do. I believe that she channeled her anger at the loss toward me, and through her pain, she lashed out.

That same month, I was doing a seminar in Long Island, and the 9/11 factor was working overtime. I had already done at least five 9/11-related readings that night and assumed my hostage situation was over . . . until I was hauled over to the back of the room. There, five kids—Marie, Kathy, Chuck, Ray, and Joey—and their mom, Rosalie, were spread out across two rows of seats with expectant, hopeful looks on their faces. As I zeroed in on them, I'm sure they didn't expect to hear the first thing that flew out of my mouth. How was I to know that I was about to reveal a well-kept family secret? Blame it on the Other Side:

> **John:** Someone here is pregnant. I have a father figure coming through who's saying congratulations.
> **Kathy:** I am!
> **Chuck, Ray, Joe:** What?!
> **Kathy:** My brothers didn't know yet!

John: You have a dad who's passed. He claims he was in uniform—like a policeman or postman or military person or fireman.

Kathy: Yes.

John: He's telling me he had a nickname like "Duke" or . . . something like . . . I see some sort of grand title.

Kathy: His nickname was "God"! And he has "Dutch" tattooed on his arm.

John: Oh, how I wish he got me to say that to you! *"God is coming through to you!"* He says his passing is recent. He's complimenting you on a wreath . . . as if there was a wreath in his honor with red and white on it. And he's claiming his sister and wife would look at his passing in the way Jack Kennedy passed. And he says his wife was stoic and strong like Jackie Kennedy. I need to compliment her for doing that—she kept everyone together. And he had a flag burial.

Rosalie: Yes.

John: He's acknowledging a celebration in May.

Rosalie: His daughters' birthdays are in May. And that's when we had his funeral.

John: I'm asking him to describe his passing, and he won't. Is he one of three boys? Or does he have three boys?

Rosalie: Both. He has three brothers . . . and he has three sons.

John: Does he have a son with him? Did he lose a son or lose someone he looked at as a son? A friend's son. Is there a Michael living?

Rosalie: That's a friend's son. And yes, there was always a joke, just kidding around, that Michael was his illegitimate son.

John: Michael was there before him, to help him over. Also, he's making me feel like he didn't get enough face time. Did this man have a really, really healthy ego?

All of them: *Oh, yeah!*

John: I don't wanna say he's cocky, but . . . he's confident. He's saying, "HERE I AM!"

Is there a reason why he wants me to go to Jersey? He wants me to go through the Lincoln tunnel. Did he get in a massive accident in the tunnel?

Marie: He was stuck in the tunnel for a long time.

John: And someone was born right after he passed. Where's the "P"? Pat. Paul.

Marie: Yes, his grandson.

John: He says there's a police officer in the family.

Kathy: Yes, my husband.

John: What does he mean that he's on the "other" team?

All (laughing): We understand that!

John: He's claiming that "J" passed.

Kathy: That's his brother, Joe.

John: He brings up his uniform again. Is it on display somewhere? He's telling me 11 . . . so that's either the 11th month, November . . . or the 11th of a month.

Rosalie: Yes, that makes sense.

John: Who has his hat? He's showing me his hat. This is a work hat.

Chuck: I have it.

John: And . . . one of you is in school. Does one of you teach something to do with balls?

Ray: Yes, I teach phys. ed.

John (to Chuck): And you have his ring, too? You have his ring in your pocket?

Chuck: Yes! [Chuck pulls out his dad's ring from his front pocket.]

John (to Ray): And what about you? Do you have the ring yet?

Ray: Not yet. My mom says I'm supposed to get his other ring, but I don't have it yet.

John (to Joey): He says your skepticism is good. That is how he would be. He also says one of you has his name.

Ray: I do!

John: He's also acknowledging Mickey Mouse. And I see a boat . . . I see fishing.

Marie: Oh my God! We're going on the Disney Cruise. We just booked it.

John: And what does he mean that they gave him a page? Someone wrote about him in a book?

Kathy: He wrote a book.

John: No, he . . . he only has one published . . . well, as far as he's concerned, it's two. And the second one can be finished. He says someone in the family has a talent for writing and can write a kickass ending. His passing seems extremely fast to me. He's going back to the wreath.

Rosalie: I just saw a wreath I wanted to get for him.

John: Was it red and white?

Rosalie: Yes. For Christmas.

John: He says your house is like Grand Central Station, with people coming and going. He puts a spotlight on your house. I see famous people coming over. I see Giuliani?

Rosalie: Yes, that's right.

John: Wait . . . your husband passed on September 11th, too?

Rosalie: Yes.

John: He's pulling me forward . . . I think there's going to be a "me, too" connection coming up. . . .

Deputy Chief Ray Downey, Chief of Special Operations, was a New York firefighter known across the country for developing innovative rescue techniques to save people's lives. He had directed rescue efforts after the bombings in Oklahoma City and at the World Trade Center (WTC) in 1993, and after hurricanes in the Dominican Republic. So it was sadly ironic on the day of September 11, 2001, that this time he was one of the thousands missing beneath the rubble.

Chief Downey was making his way over to the Trade Center when the first tower collapsed, stalling him in a tunnel en route to

Manhattan. Before the second tower came down, he had reached the WTC and had joined the rescue efforts. He was last seen running to help others as the debris from the second tower began falling.

For days after, Chief Downey's two firefighter sons—Chuck, a lieutenant; and Joe, a captain—dug through the rubble where his car had been parked in the hopes of finding their dad alive. They found the crushed car, but not their father. In the car, though, was the favorite hat he always wore—a fire-department baseball cap with the words "Special Operations" on the front, which is now cherished by his sons.

Less than two months before the disaster, Downey had been honored at a party given for him at Gracie Mansion by New York Mayor Rudy Giuliani, where he was bestowed the Crystal Apple award for his contribution to the city. It was no wonder then that the guys at the firehouse called him "God"—a nickname the family didn't know about until son Joe joined the department.

"He came home one day and said to my mom that all the guys were calling him 'Jesus' because he was 'the son of 'God,'" recalled Kathy, "and that's when we discovered what they called him. He could be very intimidating because he'd accomplished so much, but my father was the first person at your side if you needed help." At his funeral, attended by the mayor and decorated with flags, "people told my mother she reminded them of Jackie Kennedy because of the way she was so dignified," Kathy said.

The whole family was shocked when Chuck stood up in the middle of the reading and pulled their dad's lieutenant ring from deep inside his pocket—no one knew he'd brought it that day. And they had a good laugh at their dad's ribbing about one family member being a cop.

"My husband was a police officer, and my whole family were firefighters, and they had that rivalry." Kathy laughed. "That was the big joke. And the funny thing is, now he's a fireman, as of last month. He graduated in April!"

Since September 11, dozens of newspaper articles have been written about Chief Downey, and tributes including scholarship funds have been established in his name. But the family would also like to continue on with his work. He had written one book, *The Rescue Company,* and after he died they discovered he'd been working on a second.

"I hope we can finish it for him," said Marie, "since he says it can be done." The Downey family always knew that their dad was special to them, but didn't realize how many lives he touched when he left for work each day.

"Ten thousand people came to his funeral service," recalled Marie. "We were amazed. They closed the schools in town, they closed the roads. It was overwhelming. And so was the reading we had. We left the seminar that night feeling differently about 'death.' It doesn't bring him back, but to know he's still there somewhere makes our hearts feel good."

And just to top off the evening, the Other Side went for number eight. I was pulled over to another family, two sisters, sitting in the front row . . .

> **John:** I'm being pulled over here . . . who's the Jeff?
> **Woman:** That's with me.
> **John:** Someone passes from an impact. And I think . . . wait. You have a 9/11 connection, too?
> **Woman:** Yes.
> **John:** I'm getting a feeling of honor. So he was working? Was he a fireman?
> **Woman:** Yes.
> **John:** And . . . they called him in the bombing in 1993, too, right? He was there the other time, he's telling me.
> **Woman:** Yes.
> **John:** He wants me to say "Tiger."
> **Woman:** Another fireman he worked with, that's what he called him.
> **John:** And who's Nick?
> **Woman:** That's him . . . that's my husband.
> **John:** Wait . . . and . . . [to the woman sitting beside her] . . . *you* have a 9/11 connection, too?
> **Woman #2:** Yes.

At this point, the rest of the room could barely contain themselves. The atmosphere was so highly charged that everyone was sitting on the edge of their seats.

John: He's acknowledging a "Kate" or a "Katey."

Woman #2: Kitty. We have an Aunt Kitty who's passed.

John: He says there's a male one level above who's with him.

Woman #2: Uncle Ben.

John: He says that when the terror attack happened . . . you knew he'd be gone. . . .

Woman #2: I knew. I knew it when he called me.

John: He called two people. Wait [to the two women] . . . you two are related?

Woman #2:: Yes, she's my sister-in-law. I lost my two brothers.

John: They were literally together? In the same building?

Woman #1: Yes.

John: One of them is making me feel like . . . your mother, she'd be fine if she didn't wake up tomorrow.

Woman #2:: She's a very spiritual person, but she's tired. . . .

John: Your mom lost two other children before this. I don't know if she had two miscarriages?

Woman #2: I know she had one for sure.

John: I'm getting that there are five kids in the family.

Woman #2: Yes.

John: He wants me to acknowledge Ted.

Woman #2: My brother, Ted.

John: And what's your Pennsylvania tie?

Woman #2: My mother lived in Pennsylvania.

John: Where's Julia? Julie?

Woman #1: Julie, that's me.

John: They're okay. They were very high up in the building, right?

Woman #1: Yes. On the 95th floor.

John: They passed very fast. On the phone . . . did he say something to you like he was afraid?

Woman #1: He said to me, "It doesn't look good. This is bad."

John: Please, please know that they're okay.

A 9/11 passing is no different from any other passing to the people left behind. Each person who has lost a loved one experiences their own personal tragedy, and we all must find a way to deal with the loss and grief. I would hope that in dealing with that grief, you would honor those around who are trying to help you through it. And if a loved one on the Other Side attempts to make contact with you, please don't dismiss the experience. They're reaching out with love, and if you respond with anger, you'll cut off the communication because they'll see that you're not ready and willing.

Yes, it *is* important to have certain expectations about the process . . . and that means you should expect solid validations that will assure you that it is indeed your loved one coming through. At the same time, you can't expect only validations that *you* decide upon to come through—and if they don't, decide the process isn't real. That's like going to a concert and expecting a performer to sing only your favorite songs, and when they don't, deciding that the concert didn't exist at all.

As this generation becomes more aware of the open lines of communication between our world and the next one, you yourself will become more a part of this process. I think that talking to our loved ones on the Other Side on a daily basis—and without the use of a medium—will become commonplace.

WHEN I THINK OF THE SPIRITUAL EVOLUTION we've already seen in the last few years—the drastic changes in societal views about life after death—I can't help but think of Shelley, who would have flourished in this new environment. Her death was a major personal and professional loss for me, and when she died I couldn't understand why God would take such a gifted medium and teacher who could have helped so many more people here in this world. But now, I wonder if God took her so she could expand her work elsewhere. Remember when I said that Shelley was always the queen of the "Greeting Committee" here on Earth? Well, I believe that Shelley is still acting as the Greeting Committee, but on the Other Side.

Shelley died two months before the attack on the World Trade Center, and the timing of her death is uncanny to me. The way I figure it, she crossed over, had a few weeks to acclimate herself, and then she got to work doing what she does best—acting as Grand Dame of the Greeting Committee. And trust me, if your loved ones needed to be met on the Other Side, they couldn't be in more loving hands. It's not a coincidence that Shelley passed when she did, and it's also not coincidental that a TV show like *Crossing Over*, which deals with death and communicating with our loved ones, was put on the air one year before such a tragedy. I think it was part of the Universal plan, to prepare the consciousness of our country for what was to come and what we would need to endure.

And to be a part of that preparation and healing has been the greatest honor for me.

CHAPTER NINE

Mama Mia!

MY MOTHER LEFT THE PHYSICAL WORLD NEARLY 14 YEARS AGO, and I still hear her talking to me almost every day. I don't mean I hear her in the "psychic" sense, but in the regular mother-son sense. Her love and parenting are so deeply ingrained in my soul that I hear her teaching words and sometimes just her Mom-like remarks ringing in my ear as I go about my daily routine.

Especially now that I'm a dad, I experience flashbacks of my mother from my childhood—songs she sang to me, funny voices she used in order to amuse me (she'd make me laugh by doing Ernie's laugh—of the Bert and Ernie duo on *Sesame Street*). I consider all these small moments validations that my mother is still with me.

The reading in this chapter, with model Mia Tyler, demonstrates how one mother's love and connection to her daughter is still strong and very much alive on the Other Side. When we began this book, Natasha immediately thought of Mia—daughter of Aerosmith's Steven Tyler and sister of actress Liv Tyler—as someone who would be interested in this process.

As usual, I had no idea whom I was reading the day I walked into the hotel suite in midtown Manhattan. And, since I'm not a subscriber to *Vogue* magazine, I didn't recognize Mia on sight. Arriving 30 minutes late, I was met at the door by Natasha's smiling and excited face, and my first thought wasn't about the "client" I was about to meet, but about Natasha. She'd organized this session and felt a sense of obligation, which the planner of a reading often takes on—as if they're responsible for who comes through during the session (when even the psychic cannot take on that responsibility!). And there was something else on my mind. Ever since we began this project, and particularly since I discovered in our earlier reading with Norris Mailer that Natasha had lost her own mother, I'd been seeing that the sessions were having a personal effect on her. Especially during readings involving mothers and daughters, it was as though she was vicariously experiencing a reading herself, and hearing her own mother's words of love and validation.

That has always been true for me, too, with each and every one of the thousands of readings I've done. I've always maintained that I do this work selfishly, because with each connection I make for a stranger, I'm indirectly validating for myself that my own loved ones are alive and well on the Other Side.

Mia came to the reading with her cousin, Julia, and as I found out after the fact that she (Mia) was hoping to connect with *her* mother, who had passed away six months earlier. Mia's reading is an example of a daughter finding out her mom is still watching over her—and a reminder to us all that our parents look out for us even after they're gone.

John: I've got an older female coming through that I'd look at as being either a mother or being like an aunt or a grandmother. The connection is intense. And the emotion that comes up around this feels split, as if there's a dual type of relationship, where two people are within one in some way. And I feel like it's something that has unfinished business attached to it.

Now, I don't know if there's a connection to some-body who crossed themselves over, where their actions bring about their passing, but there's somebody who's claiming that they're responsible for how they got there.

I'm being shown drums, so I don't know if there's some type of drum connection to this woman, if there's a drum relationship to you, or it's you. But they're bang-ing on drums for me. It's a way of either telling me that somebody is known for their drums, somebody has the drums, somebody's taking drum lessons, somebody's a drummer, but there's a drum reference that they want me to come up with.

Mia: Should I tell you what—

John: Nope, nope. This woman who's claiming to be like the mother has a male figure to her side who's with her. So, this is actually a biological mom that we're talking about?

Mia: Yes.

John: Then I'm talking about either her brother, a brother figure, or somebody who would be on the same level . . . an uncle or another male figure like that who's with her.

Mia: Okay.

John: Now, I just want to say something else, and I'm sorry to say it like this, but there's an issue of abuse that comes up here in a big way. So I feel like I don't know if this is physical abuse or sexual abuse, but there's a lot of abuse here.

Mia: Yes.

John: This is connected to your mom?

Mia: Yes.

John: I think she feels that there were dead ends in places for her. And, I don't know if she gave you up, or if she chose not to raise you, or if she chose to shirk respon-sibility of being the nurturing, maternal energy that you would like to convince yourself you had—

179

Mia: Yes.

John: But she's making me feel like, you need to understand that we both know you didn't have that, okay?

Mia: Yes.

John: But she wants you to know that doesn't mean that she doesn't love you. And it doesn't mean that she doesn't look at you as being a friend, because I think she does. And I also feel like your connection to her is probably even stronger now than it was when she was here, and that she has influenced your creativity, and she's influenced your self-worth. So I feel like you actually now look at things in a very, very different way.

Mia: Yes.

John: She knows that in her death she's altered your life in the biggest way possible, but you have to know that that doesn't come without paying a price. And the price is huge. And she's making me feel like you have to understand that there are a lot of issues within your family that you won't be able to fix or control, you won't be able to get the answers, you won't be able to understand, and some things just have to be taken at face value, and you have to know this is what it is.

Mia: Yes.

John: Now, she's also claiming you [pointing to Julia]. So, I don't know if you're not her daughter, if you are her daughter, I don't know what your connection is to her, but she's making me feel like I need to thank you for being supportive, and for—you come across with words at times when people couldn't actually give the words. And I don't know if you guys know each other from being three years old, or if there's some type of really strong bond right underneath the age of five, like in kindergarten, or if you were split up in some way. . . .

Mia/Julia (laughing in unison): *Yes!*

John: . . . but she's making me feel like it's important for her to address that you're here. And I don't know if you're the artist or if somebody is known for their painting, or you're supposed to acknowledge the painting reference to you. Like you painted on her walls when you were a child or took nail polish and made pretty little faces on whatever this is.

I also want to tell you that she's got her mother with her. So to me there's a female figure above her I'd see as being her mother, her aunt. You're looking at me like I'm crazy, but I'm still going with this—

Mia: No, I think—

John: Wait, wait . . . let me do this. There's a unique "G" name connected to this family, so somebody might be Gloria, somebody might be Gwen, there's like a "GA" sound, there's a hard "G." But I really believe her mom passed, so if it's not her mother she's got, then I believe it's the oldest female that's with her. . . .

Mia: Yes, yes.

John: Who I believe passed before her.

Mia: Yes.

John: Who wants me to let you know she was there to greet her on the Other Side. Now, there's a magazine connection that I'm supposed to bring up connected to your mom.

Mia: Yes.

John: But I'm supposed to acknowledge the magazine connection to you *with* your mom. So does she mean she was in it? Or on it?

Mia: Yes, both of us.

John: And she's making me feel like there's one shot of your mom that looks like you, or that you paralleled her in some way.

The other thing she wants me to talk about is a frame. And she's making me feel like it's—it looks like a brassy-looking, gold metal frame, but it's not an old-fashioned frame, it's a . . . I don't know what you call it. Imagine having a frame and hammering the crap out of it so that it would have circles banged into it, like bent. She's telling me to acknowledge that.

Now was she adopted?

Mia: No . . .

John: Why would she bring up adoption? She's telling me to talk about Carol. Or Carolyn, or Kara, Carol . . .

Mia: Carol? I don't know a Carol . . .

John: Did Carol live near you when you were kids?

Mia: Well, yeah, when we were little, across the street.

John: She might want to get me to go back to that time frame. So if you try to take us back to that place—that might be where the adopted thing goes, to that time period. So at that age, when there was that Carol person around, that might be the time period when someone was either given up for adoption or that might have been the time when she took care of somebody else's child, or somebody else took care of her child.

She's showing me pink roses. That's her way of expressing her love for you. You wanted to know if she had the dog with her?

Mia: Oh, yeah!

John: She says yes.

Mia: Oh my God.

John: You have a camera of hers? She's showing me an actual camera, and it's an old-fashioned-looking camera to me. Like a Polaroid camera.

Mia: She gave me one she found. It wasn't hers; it was something she got when she was sick.

John: It might just be her way of describing what was happening around you at the time. She says to bring up October. There's gotta be a connection to October as well. And I'll tell you I think it's around the 17th. Write this down. There's a connection to October 17th. Now . . . she said you were hoping to hear from her today?

Mia: Oh, yeah.

John: I love when that happens.

She's making me feel, though, that there's a . . . I just want to go on record, you said she was sick, but she's making me feel like there's maybe a three-day period where everyone thought she was gonna be okay, or there was a three-day period where everything was fine, or there was a three-day period where she just felt awesome. Or maybe a three-day period where she was on very heavy medication and that's why she would feel awesome, I don't know.

Mia: Yeah.

John: She's telling me to talk about upstate. She wants me to tell you about upstate?

Mia: Yeah.

John: And I don't know if you're her only child? Okay, you are. Because she's making me feel like you're *it* . . . you're the world. But I don't know if she was ever really able to say that to you. I don't know if she was ever able to verbalize to you your importance. You know the feeling that I have is . . . it's very hard to describe it when they give me this feeling, but I feel if I'm your mom, I'm in awe of you.

Mia: [nods]

John: Like you're mine—I made this—how did this happen? I don't feel like I deserve this because I didn't really do this, you know, it's like I can't take credit for this. That's the feeling, that's how it's coming across to me. And there's silent praise. She wants to know if you kept the barrette. To me a barrette would be a hair tie or something that goes in the hair, so I don't know if it's something you have from your childhood or if it's something of hers that you kept. I don't think she means you kept her hair, but there's something about the barrette or the hair thing.

Mia: I don't know. I've got so much of her stuff. . . .

John: She's also telling me to talk about . . . are you going to California, are there any California connections? Because I'm hearing the song "California Dreaming" in my head.

Mia: Yeah! I'm going to move there. Is it a good thing? [laughing]

John: They'll never tell us what to do, but she's showing me that this is what's here. [To Julia:] Did you come into the city especially to do this? [To Mia:] So you're supposed to take her out to dinner tonight because of this?

Mia and Julia (laughing and in unison): Yes! We're going right after this!

John: Okay, when they do that, that's just their way of letting you know they know what's what.

Mia: We just decided this, like a half hour ago!

John: Just know that she's very happy to be able to do this. She's happy to be able to come through for you. And I don't know if you come from a Catholic background, but she's showing me St. Patrick's Cathedral.

Mia: Yeah, of course she is, yeah.

John: But St. Patrick's Cathedral is a big deal.

Mia: Yes. I was baptized there.

John: You were? Wow. Okay . . . she's pulling her energy back.

Mia's mother, actress/model Cyrinda Foxe Tyler, died on September 7, 2002, at age 51, after battling a stroke and a brain tumor, but she came through to me that day bursting with intensity and energy. "Yep, that's my mom," said Mia, "She was intense. She was a ball of fire."

Cyrinda, I learned, was born Kathleen Hetzekian, was the inspiration for the David Bowie song "Jean Genie," and was also a regular of Andy Warhol's avant-garde scene of the '60s. After Mia filled me in on her and her mom's history, the drum references I got during the reading made perfect sense. As well as Cyrinda's obvious music connection, Mia told me that her boyfriend, Dave (who became her fiancé a few months after the reading), is a drummer and that her father started out as one, and then Julia added that her father and brother were also drummers—"so there are all kinds of drummers in the family," they laughed. Also, since Mia's dad is a celebrity, it may have been a way for Cyrinda to show that connection without letting me know who Mia's dad was, thereby protecting the anonymity of the reading.

Some of the information that came through was very personal to Mia and her family. Her mother revealed the abuse she'd endured growing up, which Mia acknowledged. Linked to that abuse was Cyrinda's perception of herself as a "dual personality."

"Oh God, yeah, because her real name was Kathleen," Mia explained, "and when she ran away from home from the abuse and everything, she changed it to Cyrinda Foxe . . . so there are two personalities. She left that other person behind."

I assured Mia that her mother was going through a healing process on the Other Side about her past troubles growing up and the conflicts she had as a mother. "I'm glad she acknowledges what she did here and that she doesn't feel that way there," Mia replied. "As sad as I was to watch her suffer, I kept saying after she died that she's in a better place, and maybe she's not feeling all that there. That was the one thing I wanted to know . . . if she's still angry or not, and since that was the first thing you said, it makes me feel a lot better."

The girls were also giddy that Mia's mom came through with their own spotted history. The two of them, Mia and Julia, had been very close as little kids and then were separated for many years and lost contact until Mia tracked Julia down again. Since their reunion, the two have been as close as sisters, which came through in the reading as well.

Mia's mother also picked up on a lot of events happening in her daughter's life today, such as her upcoming move to Los Angeles from New York to jump-start her music career, and a recent photo shoot that was a special nod to mom.

Mia recalled, "I just did a thing in *Vogue* magazine where I'm wearing this outfit, and I've been saying for weeks that it's the exact same outfit she'd wear and that she would *love* it if I was in this outfit because it's *exactly* how she wanted me to dress. And I keep saying, 'That's her!' It's me, but it's also her."

Both Mia and Julia have felt Cyrinda's presence around them since she passed, and asked me if some of the "strange" occurrences—a missing phone, a temperamental, flickering stove—were her ways of trying to communicate with them. I checked in with my guides, who were still keyed in to Cyrinda's energy, and asked them. "No, she didn't do any of that," I told them, "but . . . she *will* take credit for the computer thing. . . . "

At that, the two young women got excited. Mia explained that right after her mom passed, she was in Chicago with her boyfriend, and his computer kept going on and off as she was thinking about her mother. And then, in our discussion, she discovered yet another computer communication.

"Oh my God . . . there was something else I never even told you," Julia excitedly told Mia. She described how she and her boyfriend were at their computer late one night when all of a sudden he looked at the screen and saw words there that he didn't write. "It was your mother talking to me!" Julia also promised to print out and send the message to her cousin as soon as she got home.

One validation Mia was hoping to hear, but didn't, was a reference to a necklace she'd brought with her that day. Her mother had sold most of her jewelry when she ran out of money at one point, but had saved one favorite necklace that Mia had inherited. Mia pulled the necklace out of her pocket—it had a coin-sized golden mandolin player on the end of the chain—and as soon as I saw it, I recognized the hammered metal with the little circles on it.

"That's what I was seeing in the reading . . . when I described the frame . . . it looked like this!" I exclaimed. I asked Mia if she'd ever hung the necklace on the edge of a frame and, indeed, she's kept the necklace hanging on a frame in her bathroom for months. It's the first thing she sees every morning. Mia was very thrilled by this final validation, and the fact that her mother was not alone on the Other Side. The male figure who came through to her side who might be the one who crossed himself over, she suspected, was Mom's old pal, singer Johnny Thunder, who'd died from an overdose in 1991 at the age of 38.

"She always said he was waiting for her; she knew he was waiting," Mia recalled. Also on the Other Side keeping mom company is Mia's childhood pet, a German shepherd. But most of all, Mia was heartened to know that her mother had let go of old, angry feelings from her past. "I just wanted to know that wherever she is, she's not bitter . . . she's happy."

Before we left each other, I told Mia that while I was driving to the reading that day I'd gotten stuck behind a bus painted with a giant advertisement for the Broadway play *Mamma Mia!*, so I should have known I had an appointment with a Mia and her mama.

"I was her baby." Mia smiled. "She would always call me 'my baby, my baby.' She would definitely always say I was her world, and she was definitely in awe of me."

With Mia's reading, we can see that even though our loved ones may have been troubled and in pain in this world, they find peace on the Other Side. And they send that peace our way, too, trying to heal relationships they have with us and trying to give us the strength to face our own challenges. With the support they send us, we can carry on in directions they may not have been able to. So in a sense, we continue to take their unfinished dreams forward, as well as our own.

After the reading, Natasha and I were both in that missing-Mom mode once more, but we were also elated that Mia had left the hotel room that day certain she'd connected with her own mother. "She wanted it so badly," Natasha told me. "I was afraid it wouldn't happen."

Judging by Cyrinda's intense energy during the session, I told Natasha that she was obviously very ready to come through for Mia. And her daughter was prepared and eager to hear encouraging, healing words from her mom. It was the right time for both of them.

CHAPTER TEN

Papa, Can You Hear Me?

WHEN SANDRA AND I DISCOVERED THAT SHE WAS PREGNANT in January 2002, thanks to the granny in Vegas, we were overjoyed. I had always wanted to be a dad and imagined having a big, loud brood of kids sitting around the kitchen table. Maybe it's because I was an only child and had always wanted brothers and sisters, or maybe it's because I loved every second of the large, crazy Italian family that has surrounded me my whole life.

Before Justin was born, I tried to imagine what kind of father I'd be, and there was one thing I knew for sure: I didn't want to be a father like mine—emotionally distant. So since the day Justin was born, every morning and night I hold my little "monster"—as I affectionately call him—and whisper into his ear, "Daddy loves you. Daddy loves you, Justin. . . . " These are words I never, ever heard from my own father.

Throughout my entire life, the relationship between my father and me alternated between two extremes—turbulent and non-existent. Most people outside my family don't know this, because I never speak about him in public. While many of you can probably recite ad nauseum the family stories I've told over and over in my books and on *Crossing Over* about Mom's side of the family, I'm sure you've noticed that I don't mention Dad or his side. At one seminar a few years ago in San Francisco, a woman in the audience stood up during the question period and asked me why I never mentioned my dad . . . did I even have one?

Well, yes and no, I told her.

For years I've kept quiet about our lack of relationship for fear of embarrassing him. But it has become more difficult to keep it under wraps with reporters wanting to unearth some juicy, scandalous tidbits about the man who talks to the dead. How about this one: In the last seven years, I've barely had one conversation with my own father. Now, I know what many of you are thinking: How can I preach about communicating, appreciating, and validating the people in your lives when I don't do this myself? Simple: I believe you should try as best you can to value your family and friends, but I also believe that if you've tried your utmost and the relationship remains unhealthy for you, you should let it go.

My father, Jack, was known to most people as one of the most honest, loyal, respectful people you would ever meet. To the outside world, he was a great guy. But to me, he was an emotional stranger. I heard for years from other people that my dad loved me but had a difficult time demonstrating his feelings and couldn't show it. My mother and father would constantly argue about his lack of emotional support for me, his only son. When did our relationship go wrong? Well, to be honest, when I was born. Part of me thinks I was born too quickly into my parents' young marriage—within their first year together.

Perhaps my father wasn't ready or emotionally equipped to be a father at the age of 26. Or maybe he resented the attention my mother gave me and took away from him. But I also believe that my mother didn't allow herself to fully detach from her somewhat overwhelming family. They were a tight-knit group, always into everybody else's business and very open, whereas my dad's family was very quiet and didn't discuss anything.

In the midst of this rambunctious Italian family, my father stood alone, the odd man out. My dad's background was Irish—which is kinda like the opposite of Italian when it comes to expressing emotion. How the two sides communicated was worlds apart: Mom's side wore their hearts on their sleeves; Dad's side kept them tightly sewn up. To top it all off—and I know I'll be pissing off many people in his family for revealing this—my father wrestled with a severe drinking problem.

As long as I can remember, he had two personalities—the one that was *not* drinking and the one that *was*. Unfortunately, the one that *didn't* drink wasn't a communicator. My father was a New York City police officer and a career military man who had a strong demeanor that came across as almost gruff. He would often make my mother cry, and then she had to tell me, this five-year-old kid, not to be angry at Daddy for making her cry. I heard at least once a day that my father loved me . . . from my mother. She would constantly tell me that I had to be understanding of him, and patient, that he just could not be like her brothers, who would hug me and play with me and throw me over their shoulders.

When the *other* Jack showed up—the *drinking* Jack—it was a little different. His eyes would be a bit glassy, and his speech a bit slurred, but he would be more attentive to me. Still, I always shunned that Jack because he scared me. I would run to my room and close the door, praying that he wouldn't come in. At night, when my parents thought I was sleeping, I would hear my mom complain to him about how he should tell me he loved me and not just stare at me while I was sleeping. Apparently, he would come into my bedroom and watch me sleep, amazed that I was his. One night I woke to find him petting my hair, and I remember smiling and then rolling over, wishing he'd continue. But then left.

THE GAP WIDENS

MY PARENTS SEPARATED WHEN I WAS IN THE SIXTH GRADE, and my mother and I went to live with my grandmother in Glen Cove to save on rent. I'd come home for lunch every day and watch soap operas with my grandmother and eat leftover macaroni and meatballs smothered in warmed-up gravy. (I don't mean to offend other Italians out there, but in my house, the red stuff simmering in the pot all day was called "gravy," not "sauce.") I was an independent kid who never wanted to accept an allowance from my mom because I saw how hard she worked and didn't want to contribute to her burden. So from age 12 on, *I* worked—nabbing my first job at a local hair salon, Foxy Lady, as a "go-fer" boy. I would go for coffee, tea, bagels, dry cleaning—whatever they wanted, I went and got it.

Because of this job, I also never had to go to my dad for money, which exasperated him. He told me once that he was always waiting for the day I'd come to him and need him for something. But I'd inherited his stubbornness. I never wanted to ask him for anything, especially cash, because I always knew that the price for asking would be too high.

Besides his problem with alcohol, another major issue I had with my father was that he attached "conditions" to everything—nothing happened in his life unless it was on his terms. If I asked for help (which I rarely did), it was a big production. Yet he was always there for his friends, whether it was some police buddy who needed a favor or a friend with a military training camp who needed Dad's expertise. My father helped other people but was absent for my mother and me.

When I was in elementary school, I took my Uncle Joey to Father-and-Son Day because Dad was busy at a military meeting. He didn't show up for any of my piano competitions or recitals either—I'm guessing because they weren't macho enough for him. Ditto with my high school graduation. Like that lady in San Francisco, the other kids I went to school with didn't think I *had* a father—just a mother and a grandmother.

I remember the one time I gave in on the money issue, and only served to prove myself right. I was about 14, and VCRs had just became popular. My Aunt Theresa, my mother's older sister, was one of the first to buy one from the local video store. By this time I'd graduated from my job at the beauty salon to washing dishes at the nearby deli, a definite promotion. Even so, I knew I couldn't afford a VCR on my own.

Aware of what a TV and movie buff I was, Aunt Theresa convinced the manager of Video Quest to purchase one wholesale for me if I wanted it. The cost? Only $700 (it's hard to believe you can buy one today for something like 50 bucks). Well, it might as well have been seven *thousand*. I was making $3.35 an hour scrubbing plates for 20 hours a week, so it would have taken me more than a year to save that much. My mother had a job as an executive secretary for Columbia Ribbon and Carbon, and while her paycheck put food on the table, it wasn't enough for such luxuries.

"Johnny, I'd love to buy it," my mother told me, "but we can't afford it." And then she said it: "Why don't you ask your father?"

There she goes again, was all I could think—trying to get me together with Dad any way she could. There was no way I was going to ask him to buy it for me. But after much thought, I decided I'd ask him for a loan. I figured if I was paying him back, he couldn't hold it over my head. It was one of the only times in my life I ever asked him for anything at all. I called him up, gave him my big pitch, and was shot down.

He told me he'd only lend me the money if, after he had a "meeting" with his three other siblings, they all agreed I was "worthy" of the loan. No joke. Well, all my 14-year-old brain could register at that moment was the word *worthy,* and I felt empty inside. I was standing in my grandmother's kitchen, with the receiver to my ear, silent and numb. And when I could finally speak, I thanked my father for teaching me an important lesson that day: to never ask anyone for anything ever again for as long as I lived.

I can only think of one occasion when my father did something for me that was completely unconditional. In my junior year of high school, he showed up unannounced on my doorstep dangling a pair of car keys . . . for me. On the driveway was a cherry-red, second-hand 1979 Chevette—a gift I was not expecting and, of course, didn't ask for. He handed me the keys to this old, beat-up car—which to me was as precious as a Mercedes-Benz—and on the key chain were the words *My Keys.* He asked me if I understood what that meant, and I nodded yes. He didn't want anyone else driving this car—it was mine. And for once, his "condition" wasn't a control issue. He wanted this to be something special between the two of us, and also, he was concerned for my safety if someone else was at the wheel.

I got in the driver's seat with my dad in the passenger seat beside me, and I turned on the ignition. Before I stepped on the gas pedal, he put his hand on my shoulder.

"Son . . . *be careful,*" he told me, " . . . and never let the gas gauge get too low." And with that advice, we took a spin in my new wheels. We drove around for hours—to the beach, to the McDonald's drive-thru for lunch, across town and back with the windows open and the wind whipping against us. It was so great. To this day, I still have my keys on that key chain because it symbolizes the only time I ever felt us really connect . . . and I cherish it.

When my mother was near the end of her battle with cancer, she left the hospital to spend her last days at home. About eight of her ten siblings came over to see how my mom—and their mom (my grandma)—were holding up. In the midst of this family congregation, in walked my dad. He saw what looked like this big family meeting, pulled me aside, and demanded I speak with him upstairs in my room *in private*. It was the first time in my entire life that I thought he was going to hit me; he was furious because he felt left out once again.

By this stage in the game, I wasn't really sleeping or eating much and didn't have an ounce more of energy or patience in me. After what was probably the biggest, loudest argument we ever had, he stormed out of the house. The next few days were tough, and every morning and night my cousin Roseann (Little Ro) came over to help me take care of my mom—feeding her, bathing her . . . everything.

One night the phone rang and it was my dad's sister, Gwen. I'd like to say she was calling to find out how my mom was doing, or even me for that matter, but that wasn't the case.

"I just want you to know that if your father goes back to drinking over this, *it's your fault. . . .* "

"What are you talking about?"

"I just spoke to him, and he told me what happened at your grandmother's house, and—"

In total shock, I cut her off mid-sentence. "The only person I have a responsibility to is the woman who's in the next room dying, and to her mother, my grandmother, who's watching this take place. My father is an adult and will have to act accordingly. This conversation is *over*." I slammed down the phone.

CYCLE INTERRUPTED

MY MOTHER LEFT THIS WORLD on October 5, 1989, and up until the end, she was hoping that I'd mend my relationship with my dad and his family. So I continued to try, but I kept getting blindsided. In one of our last conversations, my father telephoned and began with, "Congratulations! I'm a new uncle . . . what does that make you?"

"Uh . . . how about *confused?*" I answered. "Did someone adopt a baby?"

"No . . . no one was adopted," he said. "My sister had a baby boy! Isn't that great?"

"Are you kidding me?"

"Why would I joke about that?"

"You're calling me up to tell me that she gave birth? What happened to the phone call . . . oh . . . I don't know, maybe six months ago, announcing the fact that she was expecting?"

"Well, it's her business," he said.

"Ookaaaaaay, then, if I wasn't good enough to know about it then, why am I good enough to know about it *now?*" I don't think he kept the pregnancy news from me to hurt me or ignore me on purpose. But what I was feeling was a big buildup of so many frustrations, and it was all linked to the way his family dealt with everything—under wraps, shrouded in secret, don't discuss it.

And I was also feeling like that teenager again, being told I wasn't "worthy" enough.

My father immediately became defensive and went on the attack. He claimed that my mother was too possessive of me as a child and because of her, I never truly understood the way "his" family thought and acted. He told me I was too Italian.

"Too Italian?!" I repeated. Who knew there could be such a thing? His attack on my mom's parenting skills and half my heritage sent me into orbit. We went a few rounds on the phone until The Boys butted in and started feeding me information. (Recently, my guides had started to show me insights about my dad and our relationship.)

"Wait! Stop! I have to say something," I told my father. "My guides are shedding some light on what's happening here, and I want to tell you—"

"Your *what?*" he interrupted, in an Archie Bunker-ish tone. He wasn't amused.

"My *guides*," I repeated, with pride. "The unseen energies that work with me when I do my psychic work, remember? *Your son is a psychic medium.* He talks to dead people." I said it as if I were speaking to a deaf person, very loud and very deliberately, and also very sarcastically.

Ever since I'd begun this work, my father hadn't been supportive of it—he wanted me to follow in his footsteps and become a police officer. In my early 20s, when I was doing psychic readings as a sideline while working as a phlebotomist, he wondered why I was wasting my time. So when I decided to pursue my abilities as a medium full-time, all he said was: "Just don't use my name." Which is why I never used my original last name, McGee—Dad didn't want me to "tarnish" his good name, so my middle name, Edward, became my last name professionally—and now personally.

"And *what,*" my father continued to ridicule me, "do these *unseen scholars* have to say?" I took a deep breath and told him what I was shown.

"They show me . . . you . . . on the phone arguing with *your* dad," I told him, "and then he died. Then they showed me the arguments you and your mother had at night on the phone. I used to ask Mom all the time why you and Grandma fought like that, and why you spoke with her like that, and Mom tried to minimize the fighting. . . ."

There was silence on the other end of the phone line. I knew he hated how personal I was getting, but I wasn't about to stop.

"And after Grandma died, the arguments were turned to home. You and Mom argued all the time—day, night, weekend . . . it was constant."

"I *loved* your mother," Dad insisted.

"I don't doubt you both loved each other," I replied. "I think that was clear. But after Grandma died, Mom was next in line for you to argue with. And now that she's gone, it's me."

My guides showed me that, because of how my father was raised, he needed to create conflict with someone to feel that he was relating to them. Unfortunately, the person he'd be "relating" to would end up wanting to choke the crap out of him. I told him all this, and made it very clear that this pattern of conflict was stopping right here, and if he wanted to have a relationship with me, I had my own communication rules and they were simple: "Respect me and treat me like the adult I am. Let's try to have a friendship."

Silence.

"You're just as sick as your mother," was my dad's response, "and I should have taken you away from her and her family a long time ago." *Click.*

If my guides, or even my mother, were trying to transmit messages from above on how to mend this painful relationship, our lines were sure getting crossed.

In light of the above, the big question on everyone's lips when I was planning my wedding a few years later was would I invite my dad? Yes, I invited him and his family—I wanted them there, if only to honor my mother's wishes and have the family together. Unfortunately, none of them responded to the wedding invitations. I remember talking about this with my cousin Phyllis. I told her that not only did I think they wouldn't come, but I knew they wouldn't even respond, and they proved me right. Phyllis was so baffled by their actions that I had to laugh.

"Now you finally understand what I've been talking about," I told her, "but my father will just say I didn't give him or his family proper respect for one thing or another, and that's why they're not coming." Phyllis, not the shy type, telephoned my father shortly after the wedding to get to the bottom of it. When he answered the phone, she asked him point blank why he hadn't come to the wedding. His response was verbatim what I'd guessed he'd say à la Rodney Dangerfield: *No respect, can't get no respect.*

I didn't talk to my father for years after that. I'd finally decided, as I mentioned earlier, that the relationship was too toxic to continue. No matter what my mother's hopes were for us, our relationship seemed too messed up to fix—at least, not in *this* lifetime or on *this* plane. We couldn't seem to get it right. Trying to work it out was more painful than beneficial, so I let it go.

Or so I thought. Three years ago Sandra got into a heavy discussion with two of her female friends—students at her dance studio—who are psychologists. The topic for that afternoon's Girl Talk session? John and his profound "dad issues." Both of these women had seen *Crossing Over* and noticed I rarely mentioned my dad or his family in my endless homespun anecdotes. In fact, they pointed out, Sandra and I barely mentioned my dad or his family even in conversation among friends. "John has a lot of father issues to resolve," they told her, in that serious-toned, therapist-speak.

When Sandra got home that night, she relayed their professional opinion to me over dinner, and I have to say, their comments really bothered me. I'd worked hard on these so-called issues, and as far as I was concerned, I'd reached a pretty good place about the whole thing, thank you very much. My dad and I kept our distance, and it worked fine for both of us that way.

I knew that my father followed what was happening in my life through the show and my media appearances and had come to respect my work somewhat. We e-mailed sporadically, and when Miss Cleo, the infamous 1-900 psychic hotline lady, was embroiled in all that scandalous fraud and court trouble, my father sent me an e-mail saying he hoped people wouldn't lump me into the same category as *her,* since I was providing a service that helped people, and not ripping them off. I had to pick myself off the floor after reading *that!*

Then there was the time I was paged off the set of *Crossing Over* with an urgent message. In total "Jack" style, my father had elicited the help of the police station around the corner from our studio to get the private studio phone number. The reason? A writer from *Details* magazine who'd interviewed me had located my dad in Florida and wanted to interview *him* for the story to get the goods on this "mystery" father and our relationship—or lack thereof.

My father was frantic and didn't know what to do, but at the same time, I could hear in his voice how excited he was that this journalist wanted to talk to him. I told him to do the interview if he wanted, but that the intrepid reporter would probably ask him about things he might not want to discuss—namely, the difficulties in our relationship. And I told him that the reporter would most likely also ask about the development of my psychic abilities—one of many questions my father wouldn't be able to answer since he wasn't around for that . . . or for a lot of things.

My dad decided not to do the interview, later telling my Aunt Theresa that he didn't want to do anything that would hurt me or my work. Each e-mail he sent to me, he signed "Daddy," and that felt a bit strange. There was still a thin, thin thread between us that hadn't been severed yet—which held the promise of one day getting stronger. But at this point, I felt that I'd dealt with our past and was beyond it all.

FATHER TIME

TWO NIGHTS AFTER SANDRA TOLD ME about her therapist friends' diagnosis of my lingering father issues, we went to see the movie *Frequency*, starring Dennis Quaid. The plot centers around the relationship between a firefighter father and his son, and how different the son's life might have been if his father hadn't died an untimely death and been absent during the kid's formative years. In a kind of supernatural *Field of Dreams* twist, the father is sort of brought back to life, and the two are given a second chance to work on their relationship.

The film really got to me, and I was mush by the time the credits rolled. Afterwards, as Sandra and I silently walked through the parking lot to the car, I looked at her and started laughing through my tears. What, she asked, was so funny?

"Not funny," I corrected her, *"ironic!"*

Watching that movie opened up a big emotional well in me and made me realize that I'd done a good job ignoring this relationship without dealing with those primal, core childhood feelings of not having a dad in my life. Even though I had my Uncle Joey and my cousin Glenn as great father figures, I didn't have a dad. And that realization hit me strong. Sandra's friends were right . . . I still had my dad issues. It was a startling realization for a grown man of 30. How was I supposed to fix this? The idea of instigating a heart-to-heart with dear ol' Dad like families do on all those *Afterschool Specials* felt totally foreign to me, and I knew that neither of us was up for any major surgery like that. We just weren't ready to deal with each other yet. We didn't have the tools to do it.

I kept my revelations at bay until two years later, when we found out Sandra was pregnant. The prospect of becoming a dad brought all those feelings up in me again: feelings of being abandoned by him, of being "unworthy," concerns that as a dad myself, the cycle would continue. Well, at least I could work on that last part by myself. I figured if I could devote myself to being a good father and explore the father-son dynamic from a dad's point of view, that would help me heal whatever issues I had, and they might transfer over to my relationship with my own father. So I vowed that I'd show my love to my son, would verbalize it, and would love him unconditionally.

During the pregnancy, I waffled back and forth with the thought of calling up my father to tell him about it, but each time I brushed it aside. I didn't want to deal with any negative stuff just yet when I was feeling so happy. Maybe later. But every month, as her belly grew, Sandra asked me the same question: *"When are you going to call your father and tell him he's going to be a grandfather?"*

At one point I told her *she* should call him. "I would," she said, "but I think you're the one who needs to do it." I must admit, I might have been delaying telling him the news because part of me wanted the satisfaction of calling him up and saying, "Congratulations! I'm a father! *You know what that makes you . . . ?*" like he'd said to me in one of our last conversations.

By the time Justin was born in September 2002, I still hadn't called my father. I still wasn't "ready." But I was beginning to understand him a bit more. I found myself staring at Justin's little face as he slept (just like Dad had) with so much awe and love, and I empathized with my own father because I now knew he must have loved me. And it must have tortured him that he couldn't show it. This realization was a start.

MYSTIC PIZZA

WITH THE NEW ADDITION TO THE FAMILY, Sandra and I settled into being Mommy and Daddy. Weekends at our house became like an Italian-Portugese convention, with tons of family and friends passing through; and lots of food, games, and loud conversation.

One Saturday night last November, we were having a pizza party with my Aunt Theresa; cousin "Little Ro" and her husband Glenn; my aunt Roseann ("Big Ro"); and the new cozy family threesome of Sandra, myself, and six-week-old Justin, when Aunt Theresa decided to get all psychic on me.

"John, look . . . all I've been dreaming about lately is dead people," she told me. "They come to talk to me about this or that. Why are they coming to me and not you?"

I laughed and told her I'd been working so much lately they were probably getting a busy signal trying to reach me and the psychic operator redirected them to her . . . *ha, ha, ha*, I laughed.

But Aunt Theresa wasn't laughing with me. All joking aside, she could be extremely psychic and often picked up on family stuff. Yes, I do believe psychic ability can run in families. In fact, I'd venture to say that *both* sides of my family have a kind of pre-genetic disposition for it—which is really ironic since my father always shunned the whole psychic world. I never knew he had other connections to it until one day, after I'd been doing this work for a few years and had decided he would never fully accept it.

My father and I were having a brief conversation about my work on the phone, and he casually dropped a bomb. "You know, " he said, just before hanging up, "I was sort of hoping that 'it' was going to skip your generation. . . ."

"What?" I said into the phone. Did I hear him right? "*What?! What are you talking about?*"

In his roundabout way, Dad all but admitted that his own mother—who had a knack for reading tea leaves among her circle of friends—had her own psychic abilities, which were frowned upon in the family and never, ever discussed. Except for seeing her on my birthday or at Christmas, I rarely saw my grandmother on Dad's side. I surely don't remember ever having any "psychic" connection with her.

"Now you tell me this?" I demanded. *"Now this comes out?!"*

It would have been nice to know earlier, that's for sure. It might have explained a lot about my own abilities and also about my father's distaste for the whole subject.

Either way, psychic ability is a family trait. So when one of my relatives tells me they're having dreams or visions or whatever, I listen. I asked Aunt Theresa to tell me more about these dreams she was having.

"Well, that's just it," she continued, puzzled. "I'm dreaming about all these dead people . . . and then I had a dream about your father last night. In the dream he was in a real rush—like he was going someplace and couldn't stay. But he specifically told me I was to call him in case there was anything wrong with Justin. Is Justin okay? And why would I be dreaming about your father?"

Big Ro, who was stacking up the empty pizza boxes, interrupted with her own psychic analysis: "John, you *did* call your father to tell him he was a grandfather, didn't you?"

I chose to answer Aunt Theresa's question first. I could explain the Other Side much easier than I could explain my relationship with my father.

"I think the energies know you're receptive to their messages," I told her, "and it's their way of letting you know they're around. But I have no idea why you're dreaming about my father . . . maybe you're going to hear from him soon. And Justin is fine." And then came the more difficult answer about my dad.

"I know I should call him . . . but I just haven't been able to do it yet," I admitted.

At that, the topic became a hot debate, with Sandra and Big Ro voting that I should call my father, and Little Ro and me vetoing the idea. "If I were you, I wouldn't call him," my cousin said. "After all, he was never around for anything else . . . why give him the honor?" Before an all-out battle erupted with me in the middle of the tug-of-war, I changed the subject and broke out the Pictionary.

At about six o'clock the next morning, I got up to change Justin's diapers and give him his first bottle, and the two of us settled into the rocking chair, swaying back and forth. It was such a peaceful moment, all alone with my son—complete tranquility as the sun rose through the curtains. Justin, on the other hand, was having an entirely different experience. He was cooing and gurgling and looking straight ahead, past me, and laughing as if someone was playing with him. I turned around and looked in the direction of his gaze, and all I saw was a wall.

"Who are you playing with, you little monster?" I asked him in baby-talk. "Justin, do you see Grandpa? Are you playing with Grandpa? *Where's Grandpa?*" I was thinking of Sandra's dad, Fernando, who lived about 20 miles away in Queens, whom Justin simply adored. And once I said it, I thought it was odd that I was asking Justin where Grandpa was. My grandmother used to say that when babies played and cooed at nothing in front of them, they were playing with the angels.

I do believe that babies are directly connected with the spirit world because they have no prejudices about the existence of the Other Side and its inhabitants. In a nervous tone, I said out loud, "Justin, Grandpa better be in Queens . . . or your mommy is going to be one upset cookie. Justin, *who are you playing with?*" But my son just nodded back into dreamland, and I thought whoever Justin's angelic playmate was, he or she would have to join him in his dreams now.

I carefully put him in his crib with his little *ShooSha* (Portuguese for "pacifier") to keep him company on *this* Side, and the phone rang. I jumped to answer it before it woke Justin.

"I know it's early," Aunt Theresa whispered apologetically, on the other end of the line, "but I thought I should call you right away. You're not going to believe this . . . but I think your father has died. . . ."

MAKING AMENDS

YOU COULD SAY THAT THE NEWS of my father's death reached me via a trail of coincidences, if you believe in them. You already know that I don't. My cousin James, Big Ro's son, had been chatting on-line with a girl he'd met the night before who lived in Florida, where my dad had moved about three years before. During the e-mail conversation, he mentioned to the girl that he was related to me, and oh, what a small world it is . . . this girl's aunt happened to work in the hospital where my dad had been a patient and had just died of complications from diabetes and throat cancer. She told my cousin that my dad's funeral was the next day.

I was a bit stunned. I hadn't "officially" known that my father was even sick, but the last time I spoke with him years before I'd felt a weird health vibe. I told him he'd better check it out, and he blew me off, telling me not to worry about it or about him. He hated when I got all "psychic" with him.

I tried the old phone number I had for my dad, but it was out of order. I called my Aunt Theresa back, and she said she had a more recent number. I called and got my dad's brother, Thomas, on the phone. Uncle Thomas said he'd called me the day before and left a message that my father had passed, yet I'd never gotten it—my voice mail just didn't record it.

My cousin Phyllis, who also lived in Florida, e-mailed me my father's obituary from the newspaper. I must say it was weird to read it. First of all, I wasn't mentioned as a surviving family member, and that final disconnection just made me shake my head. Of all the mixed emotions I felt—sadness, relief, shock—the one I felt the most was *defeat*. Reading his obituary, I had to finally acknowledge that in this lifetime I wouldn't be able to make our relationship better.

ALL OF THIS LEADS ME to one of the most important points I want to make in this book. I realized with my father's death that I was not able—and could now never—mend our differences while we were both still alive. But I also suspected that, in a strange way, with his death we might actually begin to have a relationship for the very first time.

How do I see this happening? Well, I know from my guides and from all the energies that have come through to me in the last two decades that when a person crosses over, their first task on the Other Side is to reflect on the life they've led here and understand why they made the choices they did, see how their actions affected others, and realize what they still need to work on while on the Other Side.

Our learning doesn't stop once our body does—in fact, it's probably hastened because we're no longer being dragged down by Earthly obstacles. I've said before that I see this life and the after-life kind of like school: On Earth, it's like we're in kindergarten, running around in circles and getting distracted with the toys and not knowing how to do things. When we get to the Other Side, we graduate straight to college because we immediately have more understanding, more skills, and more smarts. It's still us, but it's like a wiser, *better* us.

Now if you understand that the exchange of energies between two people doesn't stop just because the body stops, and we can continue to "exchange energy" or communicate with our loved ones even after they've crossed over, it stands to reason that if you had a troubled relationship with someone and they crossed over, and then, in reviewing their life, they learned of their misguided ways and cleared their energy of negative patterns, then you both can continue to work on and improve your relationship even though they're not standing in front of you. You may not be able to communicate in the way you used to—talking on the phone, writing letters, or meeting for a cup of coffee—but you can adapt the old ways into new ones. I often suggest to people that they sit down and write letters to their loved ones who have passed because I know they're looking over our shoulders, reading our words as we write them (the Other Side is even faster than e-mail).

And why should you stop talking to your loved ones just because you can't see them? I do believe that they can hear our words and feel our feelings, and then respond by sending us their own feelings in return. Often, we might not be aware of it. For many people, this exchange happens during dreams, or with a "feeling" that we brush off and think is a figment of our imagination. But believe me, it's happening.

One woman I know, Sandy Goodman, author of *LOVE NEVER DIES: A Mother's Journey from Loss to Love,* talks to her son every day. Jason, 18, died in an electrical accident in 1996.

"From almost day one, I began talking to him," said Sandy. "Sometimes out loud and sometimes just in my head. I needed to know he was still around and hadn't just ceased to exist. And so a ritual began. On a daily basis, sometimes three or four times a day, I would say to Jason, 'I need to hear from you. If you can't get through to me, go to someone else and tell them to CALL YOUR MOM!' "

I "met" Sandy soon after on the Internet, when she was organizing a group seminar in Philadelphia with several mediums and she invited me to participate. Although I ended up not being able to attend, we exchanged a couple of short but friendly e-mails in which we discovered, of all things, a mutual appreciation for those gooey, orange slices of candy. Little did I know that from that day onward, Sandy began telling Jason to come to *me.*

A month later, I was lying on a beach one lazy Saturday afternoon getting some much-needed rest when a young male came through to me. He gave me the names "Jason" and "Sandy." I was trying to figure out whom I knew by those names when the clincher came through: "Orange slices." And then, an urgent message: *"Call my mom!"* After searching high and low for her phone number, I called Sandy for the first time ever and told her I thought I had a Jason coming through for her. After I gave her the rest of the messages that came through to me by the pool, Sandy was ecstatic. To her, this was proof that her son indeed had heard her and continues to do so.

Six years later, Sandy is still talking to Jason. And their open lines of communication have made it possible for their relationship to continue to develop.

"Jason was not a kid you would have met and thought he was a wise old soul," Sandy explained. "He acted like your typical rowdy teenager. But now, since crossing over, he's grown, and our roles have changed. I've had to accept that he's no longer my teenage son who needs my protection, guidance, and direction. Instead, he seems to be offering *me* guidance and direction when I need it."

THIS EVOLVING OF THEIR RELATIONSHIP doesn't surprise me at all. I think once people get the hang of communicating with their loved ones who have crossed over, we'll have a new generation who will consider it commonplace to work on relationships with loved ones who are on the Other Side and see them grow. At the same time, I want to point out, as I did early on in this book, that while I encourage this building of relationships, I don't advocate creating a *dependency* on communicating with the Other Side. We're still here to live our lives and shouldn't wait for a sign just to get us out of bed in the morning. A balance of both worlds is healthy so we can resolve past issues while still living in the present.

"So many people think that once a loved one dies, the opportunity to transform the relationship they had with that person ends," says Dr. Jane Greer, author of *THE AFTERLIFE CONNECTION: A Therapist Reveals How to Communicate with Departed Loved Ones* (to be published by St. Martin's Press in October 2003). "However, in life, this person may have given all they could in terms of love and support within their own earthly limitations. When they cross over, the spiritual transformation they go through, I believe, enables them to finally give and respond on an energy plane in a way they may never have been able to do before."

In her book, Dr. Greer guides readers on how to effectively resolve their anger and form the relationship connections they couldn't make while a loved one was alive. "So if you had a troubled relationship with someone when they were here, and after they pass you have an open heart and a willingness to still mend that animosity—you can. Without a doubt, a healing interaction can still take place."

In the five months since my father passed away, I've often spoken to him out loud and in my thoughts. I ask him daily to help me avoid making the mistakes with Justin that he and I made, and I also ask him to learn from *my* experiences as a loving, understanding father. I'm certain that my father hears me. Already, I feel a different vibration between our energies . . . as if he sees and understands our relationship differently now. I feel a lessening of anger, and more empathy and compassion for him.

If you're wondering if I've had any direct, dramatic psychic visitations from my dad yet, as of the time of this writing this book I have not. But I consider my Aunt Theresa's dream a true visit from my father, and confirmation that both he and my mother are watching over their grandson from where they are. My father had already passed when my aunt had that dream, and shortly after that, Justin did have a minor health problem that needed to be treated. I believe that was my dad's way of letting me know he was (finally) aware of my son and was watching out for him . . . perhaps in a way he never could for me. (I keep teasing Aunt Theresa that she's now going to have to guest-host a few episodes of *Crossing Over*.)

But as I told you in Chapter 1, when I talked about watching my son being born and waiting for my relatives to show up in the delivery room, I've learned to stop looking for the grandiose, psychic billboard, or the big *"Surrender Dorothy"* writing in the sky, because that's not always the way it happens. Sometimes the signs our loved ones send us are subtle, like hearing their favorite song on the radio, or getting a whiff of the scent of their perfume, or the smell of their cigarettes in the air.

So if you have a difficult relationship with a parent, child, or someone who has crossed over, please know that you still have a chance to work on that relationship after they're gone. However, I'm not saying you shouldn't try to work on your relationships when your loved ones are still *alive*. Please don't wait for them to cross over, thinking that this is the easier road to take.

I tried as much as I possibly could to honor my dying mother's wish that I reconcile and have a better relationship with my dad. It just didn't work. In life, my father's soul inhabited a vehicle that had a physical ailment—an addiction to alcohol that would often overtake him. I truly believe and live by my "communicate, appreciate, and validate" mantra, but I'm not Pollyana-like about it. If something isn't working when you've tried your best, should you continue to beat yourself over the head about it? I don't think so.

I believe that now, every day, I move forward and will develop a better relationship with my father—maybe not with the *man* who was here on Earth, but instead, with the *energy* that was inside that man, which still exists. I may not be able to erase the past, like Dennis Quaid could in that film *Frequency,* and bring him back to do it all differently. But I can have a future that's more peaceful and complete where he's concerned. The major feeling I have is that the struggle between us is over—like it's disintegrated in some way, even though there are days when I'm reminded of that old struggle.

A few weeks after he passed, a friend of my father who only knew my dad's version of our relationship sent an angry letter to my office about how I hadn't been "a good son" and that I was being a hypocrite when I told people to "communicate, validate, and appreciate" their loved ones. Carol read the letter out loud to me, and I sighed. There are still little minefields planted all around me, reminders of the "old Jack" I once knew, but I'm dealing with them one by one as I walk on this journey of self-discovery and healing.

Sometimes I feel that my dad is sending me encouragement from above. Just last week I got together with my Uncle Thomas and his wife, Anne Marie, and they told me that my father was so proud of me when he was alive. He used to turn on *Crossing Over* and show me off to his friends, saying, "That's my son!"

It's funny that, just like before, my father is telling me he's proud of me through other people. But I know it's true, and I know he hears me, and I believe that with him up there and me down here, we're both trying to bridge the gap inch by inch.

When I first heard the news that my father died, I must admit that for the first time in my life I felt . . . free. Not free *of* him, but free to *love* him.

And now, he, too, is free to love me.

I really do believe in my mantra of validating, appreciating, and communicating with our loved ones while they're still here. But I also believe that we all have our human limits and can only go as far as those boundaries will allow. We can continue working on our troubled relationships after someone has crossed. By the same token, if we had a loving relationship with someone who has crossed over, that relationship also continues onward and grows in its love. Remember, your loved ones are around you and always with you. The love never dies.

After 20 years of doing this work and helping countless people (including myself) through grief, I'm still grateful for the constant validations the Other Side gives us. They occur quietly and unexpectedly, like the delivery-room moment when Justin was born and the staff uttered five names of my family who had passed. On that day, I learned to focus on life happening in front of me. And the validations also appear on a grand scale. Soon after Justin was born, I made a seemingly impossible request of the Other Side. During a meditation one night, I asked my mother to validate once again that she saw Justin and knew she was a grandmother. "If you see this happening," I requested of my mother, "send me a rosary blessed by the Vatican."

A few weeks later, I received a letter at the office from a viewer of the show. It read, "I don't know why I'm sending this to you . . . but for whatever reason, I felt I had to. Here it is."

Out of the envelope a string of rosary beads dropped on my desk. They were blessed by the Vatican . . . with a card attached to it stamped with the date they were blessed: September 25th. *Justin's birthday.*

We're all still searching for answers. But when I think of my father and my son, of my mother and my grandmother, of my wife, and of all the people who have connected with the ones they love on the Other Side, I think deep down that we already know the answer:

The circle of love goes on and on and on. . . .

About John Edward

JOHN EDWARD IS AN INTERNATIONALLY ACCLAIMED PSYCHIC MEDIUM, and author of the *New York Times* bestsellers *ONE LAST TIME, CROSSING OVER*, and *WHAT IF GOD WERE THE SUN?*. In addition to hosting his own syndicated television show, *Crossing Over with John Edward*, John has been a frequent guest on *Larry King Live* and many other talk shows, and was featured in the HBO documentary *Life After Life*. He publishes his own newsletter and also conducts workshops and seminars around the country. John lives in New York with his family.

For more information regarding John Edward, see his Website at: **www.johnedward.net**.

About Natasha Stoynoff

NATASHA STOYNOFF IS A STAFF CORRESPONDENT FOR *PEOPLE* MAGAZINE, and this is her third book collaboration following *Life's Little Emergencies: Everyday Rescue for Beauty, Fashion, Relationships, and Life* with supermodel Emme; and *Never Say Never: 10 Lessons to Turn You Can't into Yes I Can* with former Miss America and CBS sportscaster Phyllis George. Natasha has worked as a news reporter/photographer for *The Toronto Star* and has been an entertainment columnist for *The Toronto Sun*. Her work has also appeared in cover stories for *Time* magazine and Germany's *Der Spiegel*. She lives in Manhattan with her husband, journalist Stephen Erwin, and is currently working on her first screenplay.

"BRIDGES"

The John Edward newsletter, "Bridges," is a quarterly magazine-style publication that includes:

- Inspirational stories
- A Q & A "Ask John" section
- Spiritually related areas
- Reader validations and experiences
- Special subscriber offers
- Guest contributors
- Other related material

To order your subscription of the "Bridges" newsletter, just fill out the order form. In addition, as a special gift from John for purchasing **both** the book *After Life* and a *"Bridges"* newsletter subscription, you will receive three (3) *free* John Edward Appreciation Pins (a $20.70 value).

Due to overwhelming demand, you must send the original form below, not a copy:

Name_____

Street Address_____

City_____State_____Zip_____

Phone_____E-mail address_____

Check appropriate box:

❑ 1-year subscription $24.95*   ❑ 2-year subscription $39.00*
*Please include $2.95 for shipping and handling. Thank you.

*Plus 3 **Free** John Edward Appreciation Pins*

Please make check payable *(in U.S. dollars only)* to **Get Psych'd, Inc.**, and mail your order to:

Get Psych'd, Inc.
P.O. Box 383
Huntington, NY 11743

Allow 4–6 weeks for delivery.

Visit our official Website at: **www.johnedward.net**

Coming in June 2004:

FINAL BEGINNINGS: The Tunnel
(fiction)

by John Edward

$\mathcal{P}$

We hope you enjoyed this Princess Books publication. If you would like more information about Princess Books, you may contact the company through their distributor, Hay House, Inc.:

Hay House, Inc.
P.O. Box 5100
Carlsbad, CA 92018-5100

(760) 431-7695 or (800) 654-5126
(760) 431-6948 (fax) or (800) 650-5115 (fax)
www.hayhouse.com

Distributed in Australia by:
Hay House Australia Pty Ltd, 18/36 Ralph St., Alexandria NSW 2015
Phone: 612-9669-4299 • *Fax:* 612-9669-4144 • www.hayhouse.com.au

Distributed in the United Kingdom by:
Hay House UK, Ltd. • Unit 202, Canalot Studios • 222 Kensal Rd.,
London W10 5BN • *Phone:* 44-20-8962-1230 • *Fax:* 44-20-8962-1239
www.hayhouse.co.uk

Distributed in Canada by:
Raincoast • 9050 Shaughnessy St., Vancouver, B.C. V6P 6E5
Phone: (604) 323-7100 • *Fax:* (604) 323-2600

Sign up via the Hay House USA Website to receive the Hay House online newsletter and stay informed about what's going on with your favorite authors. You'll receive bimonthly announcements about: Discounts and Offers, Special Events, Product Highlights, Free Excerpts, Giveaways, and more!